Advanced Praise for

Radical Embodiment

A Practical Guide to Celebrating the Skin You're In

"I didn't want to hate my body; I just knew I did. Women worldwide have imbibed messages that drown out the innocence, curiosity, and biological wonder of living in a body filled with potential. This self-hate is a cultural control mechanism that ravages female bodies and, in some cases, results in harm or death. I lived with multiple eating disorders and body dysmorphia from ages 11–23. I healed once I discovered how to feel my feelings. Guess where they were? They were trembling in hiding within my body, waiting for gentle permission to express. Emily Wishall has been through the arduous and radical process of compassionately connecting her body story from hate to like to love. Her new book welcomes you into your body safely and patiently, giving you room to breathe, grieve and transform. If any portion of your life is silenced with thoughts of your weight, waistline or your worthiness, I encourage you to page your way through this trustworthy guide."

—**Jill Miller,** C-IAYT, author of *The Roll Model* and *Body by Breath*, co-founder of Tune Up Fitness Worldwide

"Author, practitioner, and thought leader, Emily Wishall, has taken a familiar topic and pressed the refresh button. The result in her book, *Radical Embodiment: A Practical Guide to Celebrating the Skin You're In*, is a relevant and authoritative deep dive into the way through an all-too-familiar struggle for anyone who wants to feel more alive, happier, and healthier in their body. To anyone who may erroneously think that they've read it all, nothing is new, and there is no hope for their own personal transformation, think again. Emily brings a refreshing perspective from the best possible places: her own authentic journey, plus her vast professional training, plus having helped countless students and clients. Emily has earned her stripes as a compassionate expert. Her generosity to share her story for the purpose of shedding light for others who want and need to break through makes this book timeless and urgent at the same time."

—**Rosie Bank,** author of
Health Matters: 52 Ways to Get Your Body to Love You Back

"Emily Wishall is a gift. Her vulnerability allows her readers to feel truly seen and heard. Her voice speaks like a trusted friend and lets you know that you are not alone. I believe this book will help many women connect with their bodies again. Maybe even for the first time."

—**Suzanne Hanna,** psychotherapist, founder of The Wilderness Walk

"Emily is extraordinary at guiding women into an embodied state. She can identify the subtle messages and ways we as women relate to our bodies and support us in getting aligned from within so that we can love our bodies and thrive within them. This book is a must-read to get yourself relating to your body from an entirely new perspective."

—**Kavita J. Patel,** relationship expert, creator of Soul Level Love

"I so enjoyed this book. Self-love and accepting your body are something we talk a lot about but few people actually give you the tools. One of the things I loved about this book was that Emily gives you real tools and practices that show you how to love your body. She makes specific suggestions that support your mind, body, and spirit to change how you think and feel. This book provides support for mindset and inspired action. The super simple practices at the end of each chapter gives you a true feeling of being embodied and how good that can feel. Thank you Emily!"

—**Dawn Todd,** founder of Soul Awakening Entrepreneurs

"This is a much-needed book in the world! As someone who struggled with body image for decades, I wish I had had this. A beautiful, kind, and comprehensive guide to stop fighting with our bodies for good."

—**Macy Matarazzo,** relationship coach for singles,
founder of GetSuperLOVED.com

"Emily's story is so relatable that it immediately hooks the reader in and makes you feel inspired to try out the practices. Anyone who's ever wanted to end the battle of being unhappy with her body can benefit from the down-to-earth knowledge in this book. This is an essential read for anyone struggling with body image."

—**Jessie May Kezele,** brand strategist & business coach,
founder of The Daring Fempreneur

"This is a great intro or refresher on how to take care of yourself with love and compassion. Through sharing her personal story, her experience as a healer, and the accessible practices throughout the book, Emily opens the door and illuminates the way for readers to experience how good it can feel to connect to their bodies."

—**Ali Kole,** creator of Sensually Embodied

"A must-read for anyone who struggles to fully express herself and attract the love and attention they long for. Emily does a brilliant job of showing us how to live a truly confident and authentic life."

—**Rachael Jayne Groover,** author of *Powerful and Feminine*

To my nieces, my future daughters, and any woman
who has ever been made to feel not enough
because of the way her physical body appeared.

Table of Contents

Foreword

Maybe, like me, you have spent a lifetime at war with your body.

I remember hearing that feminist phrase "the personal is political" in college and thinking immediately about the battle I was in with my size and shape, the constant feeling of unworthiness I felt in my skin. I flashed on billboards of suntanned models whose appearance I would never match. The "personal" that was my body was the site of a steady, daily, political assault. I was kept small in force and expression by a machine that wanted my power to be minimal. Decorative. Appealing to men. Too busy with my own struggle to exert any influence over the giant structures that were in charge.

I recognized this reality as did my outraged, impassioned classmates, and we wrote papers and attended rallies in protest. But flash-forward several decades, and my war with my body was raging on. I tied my worth to my weight just as I always had. I felt insufficient at the same time as I felt unwieldy and gigantic. Even as I could appreciate the bodies of my friends and cherish the bodies of my partners, I could not let go the belief that I was a failure for my physical "flaws."

Does this resonate for you? Odds are, if you are walking through this culture in a female-identified body, it does. And maybe, like me, no matter how you've tried to free yourself from this internal conflict, nothing has worked. You still spend way too much time wishing you looked differently, felt differently, were closer to some flickering ideal you could never achieve.

Enter Emily Wishall. As part of my work as an editor at Modern Wisdom Press, the publisher of the book you have in your hands, I was handed *Radical Embodiment.* And I was knocked out.

Here was an author who wanted to reach her readers by laying herself bare. Here was a woman brave enough to put on the page the moments when she felt most compulsive and unlovable. Emily was willing to tell the truth about those moments all through the day when our attention is pulled away from joy and beauty and fascination, away from productivity and creativity and generating a new world, directed instead at hating our bodies.

I saw myself in Emily, and because she painted such a rich and real portrait of herself, I saw the absurdity, and really, the cruelty, of viewing my physical form as my enemy.

I felt this author's hand. I was being befriended and understood, and I trusted her.

Then came the practices. Emily, a certified Rolfer and embodiment coach, has created a method for learning to love and inhabit ourselves thoroughly and deeply. I was blown away. Each chapter deals with a way we torture ourselves, boiled down to the "limiting belief" underlying that viciousness. To address these ways we suffer, Emily provides healing strategies that come from her expertise as a practitioner and her years of work with clients of all shapes and sizes, ages and personal histories, who have in common the pain of hating their bodies.

Throughout the book, Emily presents herself as a case study. This choice is profound. Her vulnerability runs through every paragraph, and the effect is that the reader gets permission to be vulnerable, too. We are invited to bring air and light to the troubled behaviors and ways of seeing ourselves we tend to hide from public view. The author's courage drives this book, and the author's courage inspires the reader to find her own capacity to change.

Change, in the context of *Radical Embodiment,* is not a diet. It's not a new workout plan. It is an overhaul of the way we treat and perceive ourselves. It is the fierce application of gentleness to the gaze we offer ourselves.

I don't know about you, but for me, that is a radical way of being.

It dismantles all the meanness that has been the engine driving years and years of chronic dissatisfaction with my body. It frees me to live wildly and with pleasure. It is profoundly liberating. And I am grateful.

After I'd fallen in love with her method and her voice, I was given a chance to take Emily's online course, Body Love. I joined a circle of women learning the techniques I'd read about, only now with Emily as a real-time presence and guide. It was as I suspected: We all shared the same internal nightmare and the same yearning to be freed from it. Just speaking aloud about our struggles was cathartic and offered us a feeling of community. On top of that, Emily led us through the practices I'd read in these pages, and we talked about how they felt. Doing this inner work alongside other women amplified its power. And Emily was a brilliant leader, forever attentive to our emotional safety even as she nudged us into challenges that caused us to grow.

I've come away from Emily's teachings with an abundance of new skills for embodiment. More importantly, as a result of Emily's writings and course work, I carry with me a sense that my body, this protector and vessel that has carried me through my time on this planet, deserves my most heartfelt love. Every time I return from flashes of self-recrimination or shaming to this awareness of my value, my heart opens, I find room in my ribcage for deep, wonderful, breaths, and I watch myself become of greater service in the world.

Thank you, Emily. And to you, reader, congratulations on the journey you are about to take. You deserve to feel the preciousness of the body you're in. You deserve *Radical Embodiment.*

Gabrielle Idlet

Introduction

Women, Weight, and Worth.

Our culture and society tell us that a woman's worth is based around her weight. We may intellectually disagree, but if you look at how women are treated in advertisements, you will quickly find that this is true.

In 2018, the weight loss industry in the United States netted a profit of $72 billion. That's a ridiculous amount of money. It makes sense then that advertising and the media will continue to brainwash us into thinking we are not enough as is and that we need to lose XX amount of pounds before we can truly be happy. They are making billions on our hunger to be thin. Their success is formed around the basis that you are not to be approved of, you are not to succeed, and you are to be a complacent failure if you don't first address your hideous body.

And we internalize that madness. Achieving a desired number on the scale can feel more important than earning a graduate degree. Hyperfocus around weight and physical appearance robs you of your energy, clarity, power, and joy.

My hope is that this book offers you new insight and perspective on how you get to *be* with your body. My hope is that you can release the worn-out, exhausting story of being dissatisfied with your body and, instead, feel happy and more confident in your skin.

Most of my life, I lived with the belief that I was not enough because I felt too fat. This view kept me stuck. I pushed down my needs and wants when it came to relationships. My mind was continuously buzzing with the next diet, cleanse, or exercise routine that would certainly be my magic pill and allow me to, finally, be thin and be happy and have what I want.

Through my journey, I have found that I am not alone in this struggle. Sadly, most women I know have a similar story. Yes, I know society also pressures men to look a certain way, and men have their own body image struggles, but this book is geared toward those who identify as women and who have struggled with accepting their female bodies. Regardless of how you experience yourself physically, my hope is that you will be able to gain a lot from this book and place it in your own perspective. We are all in bodies, and unfortunately, most of us have been conditioned to despise the skin we are in.

There is so much freedom and pleasure on the other side of this nonlinear journey. My passion is supporting women to shift their internal narrative from feeling like their body should be different to embracing their body exactly as it is.

As you read through these pages and work with the practices at the end of each chapter, you can expect a softening and the emergence of a gentler approach to how you view and talk to yourself. You will learn specific embodiment practices that will support you in shifting your focus from being mainly outwardly based (looking for validation from the external world) to more inwardly focused, more concerned with how you feel and what you need (looking for validation from within). This gradual transformation will invite you to approach yourself and your body with increasing love and acceptance.

I hope you're ready! I'm happy you are here.

CHAPTER 1

My Body, the Problem

Have you ever felt like because you have stomach rolls, you don't deserve the fullness of what you desire? Or as if you are less valuable than others because of the thickness of your thighs?

Girl, if you hate your body, it's *no wonder*. I mean look at society and all the crap you have been fed all your life. Every female I know has had some sort of body image issue. Whether they have felt too fat or too thin, it was "too much" of something or not enough of another thing. Every girlfriend of mine has had some sort of body dysmorphia, eating disorder, or experience of feeling inadequate because of the way her body looks.

I have worked with so many amazing women in my practice. Powerful, beautiful women. Women of different shapes, sizes, colors, and backgrounds. What I have seen, unfortunately, to be the common denominator for these women is an underlying disdain for their body. The full spectrum of disdain, from the constant annoying itch of not feeling sexy, skinny, or fit enough to the obnoxious, loud sound of nails on a chalkboard of having almost every thought that fills your brain be themed around being displeased with your body. This deeply saddens and infuriates me and has lit a fire in me to help in shifting this narrative.

Common thoughts from these women:

- I'm unhappy in my body.
- I loathe my body and think if it were smaller, if I were less fat, if I had less of an appetite, then others would approve of me, and I would be happy.
- It's my body's fault I feel as if I don't belong.
- I can't be trusted around yummy food, particularly desserts. I hate this about myself. Why can't I be disciplined and have self-control like other people?
- Why am I completely preoccupied with the following thoughts? "If only I could lose ten pounds." "Do I look fat in this?" "Does my stomach look big?" "Do they think I'm eating too much?" "Do people think I'm lame?"
- I feel disgust and shame.
- I feel inadequate.
- I'm frustrated and exhausted by this process.

What's to blame?

A huge fault lies in our society and in each one of us who supports its toxic gaze. When was the first time you remember not liking your body? Was it after someone said something to you? Was it after a certain look someone gave you? Was it after multiple moments of being told by a parent or other adult in your life to "suck it in," "stop eating so much," "eat more," or "you're too thin"? Was it after seeing a woman in a film who seemed absolutely perfect? And from that image, a glossy photo in a magazine, or a shimmering bikini model reclining across a billboard, the ideal body of the woman who had it all was created. We were taught as young girls to bow to this ideal woman and do our best to severely restrict our calories, and become that perfectly shaped girl who quietly smiles in the background. We were told to take up less space, not make much noise, and be agreeable because *that* is what creates accolades in this society.

What the hell?

Seriously.

This mode of thinking, this measuring tape, is a fraud. It is backed by a system that does not have our interest at play. It is backed by a system that wants us to feel lonely, less than, and as if we need to work *super* hard to receive the smallest acknowledgment.

This mindset we've adopted is flawed.

I absolutely hate it, and it brings tears to my eyes as I write this. And yet, time and time again, I still find myself buying into it. Looking for that validation from others of "Oh Emily, you've lost weight. Wow, you look good!"

What Is Hating Your Body Costing You?

It doesn't seem to matter what size, weight, age, socioeconomic status, or race you are. If you grew up female in the United States, you have probably sized yourself up to others based on physical appearance.

If you are nodding your head in acknowledgment of, "Yeah, I've definitely compared my body to the girl on the treadmill next to me," I am not sharing this to make you feel wrong. I want to illuminate it. When we shine light on our shadows, on the ickiness that we don't want to talk about, true healing happens. We bring our power back to ourselves and have the opportunity to choose a different thought, belief, and action.

I realize my awareness is limited by the fact that I am a white, able-bodied, heteronormative, heterosexual woman who has not had to encounter racist, ableist, homophobic, or transphobic views of my body. My blind spots may be evident, and without a doubt, whole territories of societal attitudes are directed toward women of color as well as disabled and gay women.

My hope is this book's exploration of body image challenges that run through much of female experience is useful for readers of all backgrounds.

When you hate your body, what is it you are really hating? Is it the self-loathing that comes from eating *way too much* food? Is it the continual disappointment that comes from capitulating with an unrealistic and harsh cultural standard for how you should look as a woman?

Think of all the energy, time, and money you have wasted being at war with your body. What else would be possible if you weren't always fighting with your own flesh and bones? What if, instead, your body was your ally? Imagine getting dressed with ease and not giving a second thought of "Does my stomach look big in this?" Picture going out to dinner with friends and eating as your appetite desires instead of being worried that you look like a "fat" eater. How would it feel to be content and confident exactly as you are?

Freedom from Failure

You often hear in the body image world to "accept yourself as you are."

In my opinion, that is some of the worst advice you can give people who aren't happy with their body. If you have trouble accepting yourself as you are, hearing the above instruction will make you feel guilty and as if you are doing something wrong. "Come on girl, just accept yourself." It becomes yet another "should" that you are "failing."

And if it really were that easy, to snap your fingers and accept yourself, you'd already have done it, right? But it's not as simple as shifting your mindset to being positive and accepting.

The fact is, as you begin to explore your relationship with your body, your mind will weave through the spectrum from hatred, to acceptance, to love. Making peace with that fact alone will speed up your journey toward predominantly loving your body. Perhaps you first feel more neutral about your body. From there, you can move toward body acceptance. And from there, you can experience true and honest body love. My goal with this book is to offer you support and guidance along that journey. If, in the future, a time comes when you notice thoughts or behaviors of dislike toward your body, you will have the tools from the practices shared in the upcoming chapters to interrupt that pattern and return to feeling good (or even a little bit better) in your body.

When you love your body—heck, even when you feel neutral about it—you have so much more mental space to live the life you really desire to be living. Loving your body allows you to check off those other life goals and be truly present in your relationships.

Fear Will Come Up

In my work with clients, I see a lot of common fears emerge as these women work toward accepting and loving their body. Common fears lie beneath their suffering with body image and food and are a significant part of why they are struggling to release outdated sabotaging patterns. Perhaps you will recognize some of your own here.

Fear of Not Having What You Desire

You may have a subconscious fear of never having the career you want because of the way your body looks. Maybe you have dreams of becoming an entrepreneur, increasing your income, or making a bigger impact, but your beliefs about your body being flawed continue to set you back time and time again. Or perhaps you're afraid of being alone, of never having a fulfilling relationship. So much of your energy and focus may have been about not liking yourself, it's hard to imagine someone loving you with a body that is so flawed.

Fear of Being Seen

Some of my clients subconsciously hold onto extra weight because they fear what it would be like to be seen as their truest selves. If you are underweight, you, too, may be manipulating the size of your body to feel less visible to others. Whatever your body size, sometimes it can feel safer to be rejected because of the cellulite on your thighs than because of who you *are*.

Fear of the Body-Dissatisfaction Cycle Never Ending

Many of my clients fear they will always struggle with food and body image. The journey can feel overwhelming. It's easy to get lost in those feelings and can feel tempting to give up. Your mind wants to keep you comfortable and safe, and going deeper under the surface involves risk. Knowing this will allow you to make the choice to move into fruitful discomfort instead of staying stuck in what is comfortable but unfulfilling.

Fear of Trusting Your Body and Appetite.

For years, many of us have done our best to control our appetites. You have squashed it down because, God forbid, particularly as a woman, you are seen as ravenous. Or maybe you have swung to the opposite end of the spectrum, and you compulsively overeat. This disordered eating also stems from trying to control your appetite and restrict certain foods. Either way, because you fear trusting your body, you are suffering as a result.

Fear of Change

Inviting in change and growth means facing uncomfortable emotions and the unknown. I see this fear of change come up in my clients frequently through our transformative work together. Staying the same allows for a kind of certainty and stability but changing means you have to risk letting go of who you have been and how you have perceived yourself to allow in something new.

Confidence and Joy Lie Ahead

This book will show you how to begin loving your body *now*. Please take time to do the practices at the end of each chapter. Don't skip over those. Do them. The work of releasing years of patterns of hate and disdain toward your body takes more than just intellectual knowledge. You must *know* and *experience* the information in your body, at a cellular level, which is what these practices will support you in doing.

Within the chapters ahead, I am going to share with you the seven-step process that supported me in finally being able to love my body. We will move forward together, one step at a time, toward experiencing more freedom, peace, and confidence in our bodies.

Seven main limiting beliefs show up time and time again in my work with clients, and I suspect some of them may be operating in you, too. I will help clear your blinders so you can see how and where these beliefs are halting you in your own life. Then, I will share how to break these patterns. When insecurities and triggers take a nab at you, you will have more clarity and conviction to not give in to old limitations.

Staying Stuck Sucks

Early in my journey, if I was triggered and felt lonely or like I didn't belong, I would run to the store to load up on junk food and treats then rush home to consume it as quickly as possible. I was searching ravenously. I strongly desired to feel deep connection. I unconsciously denied myself from receiving and feeling true pleasure. To fill the void I felt within me, I would placate and numb myself with the momentary pleasure of an entire pizza that I ate alone with eyes glued to the TV.

I didn't have faith that I would ever experience relief from this cycle of unhappiness. I had tried the diets, the cleanses, the bootcamps. But what was missing, what I had not yet tried, was gentleness. I had not looked within for wisdom, direction, and guidance. Instead of focusing externally for the next program or guru who promised me I would lose the ten pounds for good, I finally learned what it meant to inhabit my body, to be present within myself. The realization freed me from the years of believing my body was the problem and allowed me to experience contentment, deep gratitude, pleasure, and love for my body.

Staying stuck under the lens of hating your body is not only a disservice to you, but to everyone you encounter. It blocks you from the gifts you were meant to bring. This is why I want to support you in experiencing acceptance and love toward your body, so you can reach your full potential.

Girl, I am so excited to be here on this journey with you. As I write this, I feel my heart opening, a smile comes to my face, and a deep exhale of love and gratitude moves through me. I know what it's like to be where you are. And now I know what it is like to see my body as a resource, a dear friend, and my beautiful guide through this life on planet Earth. And it feels so freaking good!

There is so much pleasure, delight, and contentment on this side. Of course, I still have moments where I get pissy at my body, wanting her to be able to move a certain way, wanting her to be able to squeeze her ass and belly into those jeans that are way too small. I'm a woman who was raised in the '90s in the United States when diet culture was shoved down our throats. So yeah, I'm still on my healing journey. But let me tell you, I have so much more space and freedom than I ever had before.

I cannot wait for what is on the other side for you. You *do* get to have all you desire. You *do* get to feel good about your body. Hell, you get to feel *amazing* in your body, and you do not need to change a thing about your body to experience that!

PRACTICE
Lovingly Unplug

Before we begin, I'd like to ask you to make a commitment. At least thirty minutes before you go to bed, but preferably an hour, turn your phone on airplane mode. Allow your eyes and mind a bit of rest from the screen and blue light stimulation before you sleep. Then, in the morning when you wake up, don't take your phone off airplane mode for thirty minutes to an hour. Use that time for you. Do a meditation. Say a prayer. Journal. Have some juicy movement time. Commit to doing this from now until you finish this book, and if it feels good, keep on going.

It is *essential* to start this practice now. A huge piece of hating your body stems from the external world. If you start your day immediately plugged into your phone, bombarded with messages, the news, what is happening with other people, etc., it is tremendously challenging to discern how *you* feel. If you don't know how you feel, you cannot begin to know what it is you want. Hence, you begin to think you want and need things that are marketed to you throughout your day (e.g., this pill, this supplement, this diet tea). But if you make the promise to tune in to yourself every single morning and night, little by little, you will identify how you *truly* feel and what you *truly* want. This practice also strengthens your internal muscle to feel how you really feel each day, so if your body and/or emotional self needs attention, you can respond. It is a subtle but profound life-changer to notice your internal guidance earlier on instead of only hearing the voice once it becomes so loud it has morphed into pain, anxiety, or uncontrollable cravings.

As you move through this book, I want to remind you how important it is to take time at the end of each chapter to do the practice. With this commitment, slowly, surely, you'll discover the path to fully nourish and love your body.

CHAPTER 2

The Gift of Hating My Body

I remember moments I spent outside when I was little, existing without fear, concern, or insecurity. Simply being. Attempting to make friends with the birds. Playing on my swing set and communicating with my grandfathers in Heaven. I was connected. Uninhibited. Free.

Then life came about.

At eight years old, I felt fat.

It didn't happen all at once. And I don't know why it happened that year. But that's when it kicked in: my first strong taste of body concern, of unworthiness, of not being enough. I thought because I was "fat," I was not good enough. Not loveable. So, I suppressed. I shut down. My sweet, innocent, soul-connected youth slowly began to dissipate.

I'm not really sure why I decided I was fat. I remember once my grandma commenting to my mom that I was chubby. As soon as we got in the car, my mom told me I wasn't and something along the lines of not listening to what my grandma said. I think my response was something of "Oh yeah, it's all good," when really those words hurt deeply. Instead of sharing my hurt with my mom and receiving her love and care, I had an even stronger need to hold it all together and appear fine, unaffected by those words from my grandmother.

When I was in the third grade, my family had photos taken. We all wore denim. Yup, family photos of the '90s. I remember seeing them and thinking I looked like a chipmunk. My cheeks were so big, and I had a pudge in my jeans at my belly. That is all I could see: how chubby I was and how wrong I looked.

If my childhood had been one where I was oblivious to my body instead of consumed with constant thoughts of how to be and look skinnier, I would not have had the opportunity to begin the journey to knowing myself so young in life.

The Hate Was My Motivation

My discomfort within my own skin is what eventually propelled my study of the scientific, energetic, and emotional aspects of the human body. I figured the more knowledge I had, the more I could morph myself into being "acceptable."

I thought my physical body was the problem. If I could simply understand it better, if I could make sense of its anatomy and physiology, then I would certainly be able to control it. This would mean I could finally have badass arms and be worthy of self-love. I believed that by becoming an expert on the workings of the physical body, I would "naturally" fix the way I looked. Then and only then could I be happy.

Along my quest, I received my Bachelor's Degree in Exercise Science. At the time, I had the intention of going to Physical Therapy school. I felt like a fake in my undergraduate exercise science classes because I wasn't enrolled in them for my love of the human body and what it could do. I took those classes because deep down I believed learning all I could about the human body would lead to me being skinny.

A couple months before my college graduation I tried to diet and began exercising two times a day so I could be skinnier and look more fit at the ceremony. I wanted to be the fitting image of a college graduate who studied Exercise Science. I wanted to have the slender body that would be largely approved of and applauded at my graduation. I cared more about looking skinny than receiving my actual college degree.

After college, I spent a year volunteering with AmeriCorps in southern Colorado, splitting my time between a homeless shelter and a thrift store. When I first moved there, I had this idealized view of who I would become: a skinny, cute, outdoor Colorado girl. I remember hanging on to a pair of overall shorts, adorable but at least three sizes too small for me. I thought it was certain that I would lose weight and be able to fit into them by the end of the year. Those overalls became like a trophy for me. Once I could fit into them, then I would finally be acceptable.

During that year, I dealt with client cases that were far beyond my training and far beyond my emotional capacity to handle at the time. It was hard. Food, particularly lots of bread and cheese, became my solace. So yeah, I didn't end up fitting into those overalls. At the end of the year when they ended up in the donation pile, they only mocked my feelings of inadequacy.

I then moved to a yoga retreat center, Kripalu, where I lived and worked for six months. Yet again, I created an idealized view of who I would become there: six months of yoga and organic food. Certainly, this was my way to get skinny at last. My study to understand more about the human body and mind continued. I attended almost every lecture, workshop, and class, taking diligent notes, not wanting to miss a word the presenter said in case that nugget contained the secret to my skinniness. I read books, oh so many books, on mindful eating, nourishment, meditation, and the like. Surely through reading one of them I would receive my hallelujah saving grace moment.

Living at this yoga center was one of the best choices I ever made, not because I finally became skinny there, but instead because I discovered others also have that monkey mind, that internal dialogue that questions and judges them. What a relief to realize it wasn't just me and there wasn't anything wrong with me. This realization was a huge catalyst in my beginning of any sort of honest and compassionate conversation with myself and my body.

From there, I had a brief stint living between two of my sisters in Kansas City as I worked and saved money to move to Boulder, Colorado (where I still live today) to attend the Dr. Ida Rolf Institute (DIRI). Once I started school there, I knew I was going to have to walk around in my underwear as a student.

Before I dive further, let me share a bit of context to better understand why in the hell I would be walking in my underwear. Rolfing Structural Integration is a form of hands-on manual therapy working with the body's fascia with the goal of supporting the body to come back to its natural alignment. In sessions, clients walk into a safe office setting in front of their practitioner in underwear or minimal clothing for the purpose of allowing the practitioner a chance to see overall relationships in the body, noticing what is working well together and what areas could use more support. When you study to become a Certified Rolfer, you are also playing the role of client, receiving work from practicing students, and so, for brief periods, you walk around in your bra and underwear in the classroom.

This horrified me. I spent my few months in Kansas City preoccupied with how I was going to get control of this fat body of mine. I feared that if my body wasn't an appropriate and agreeable size by the time I started my studies at DIRI, my future fellow classmates and teachers would judge me. I was sure they would think less of me and could not imagine I could be a valid practitioner. As it turned out, of course, I encountered no harshness about my body from others in the Rolfing program. But I continued to wrestle with the self-judgment that ran like ticker tape through my head.

Most of my life, my main mode of existence was feeling anxious and inferior. I felt extremely self-conscious. Getting dressed used to take me oh so long. I would plan extra time in my schedule as I knew I would have to try on multiple outfits before finding one that I believed didn't make me look fat. I'd obsessively look at myself in the mirror wondering if my stomach stuck out too much. I would only wear about half of the clothes in my closet as I simply felt too fat for the others.

Emotionally, I was numb. I suppressed my feelings of loneliness and insecurity with food and TV. I was stuck. I was afraid to admit this to anyone else. I was even afraid to admit it to myself.

Transforming from that lost and uncertain girl to being the proud, confident business owner and local leader I am today has been quite a journey. I now know this journey of loving my body will be lifelong. Studying the body and mind continue to fascinate me. I am fortunate to have a career where my learning never has to end. But the initial motivator for all of it was hatred for this physical vessel, my body.

Why Am I Grateful That I Hated My Body?

This is true and yet feels harsh and strange to write: Hating my body was my greatest gift. Hating my body was my loudest story. It was the message I needed to receive from my body with enough pain that I couldn't ignore it.

I couldn't keep pushing it down. I couldn't keep bypassing the unhappiness, dissatisfaction, shame, and guilt I felt. It was all there, present in my every waking moment. For that, I bow in deep gratitude and reverence for this wise, loyal, and beautiful body because if I hadn't hated my body most of my life, I wouldn't have jumped so deeply into my own personal quest for healing and knowledge.

Hating my body is what led me to loving my body. It gave me the opportunity to develop a deep relationship with myself and really get to know who I am. Instead of trying to be smaller, instead of trying to cave in on myself, I began little by little to allow myself to embody my physical form. I did this with support from multiple incredible facilitators and practices, one cell, one body part at a time. Instead of popping out of myself, stuck in spirals of negative self-talk and endless hunts for the next diet ""fix," which left me feeling invisible and not appreciated, I learned how to inhabit my body, which in turn has me feeling more seen, connected, and understood.

Feeling anxious and inferior is no longer my predominant dialogue. I feel comfortable, confident, and happy in my body. Not having those obsessive thoughts frees up so much mental space in my brain, leaving me with more energy. My focus has shifted from being primarily attentive to the external world and how to receive its approval to my internal world and how to receive my own approval.

What's the Secret to Full-on Body Love?

I'm kind of a bummer here because there is no secret.

There wasn't one *thing* that did "the trick" in my transformational journey. It wasn't one effort that changed my disdain for my body into love. It took multiple and continuous investments to get where I am today. Some of these included Rolfing Structural Integration, receiving loads of coaching, the Art of Feminine Presence Workshop, therapy, a consistent meditation practice, and multiple personal and professional development trainings.

All these supports were useful. They were needed and valuable. However, because they happened sporadically, my ability to create actual lasting and significant change to get free from that stuck, insecure place took a long time. You may be slogging through your own version of a lengthy effort to bring about change. I want to save you time.

I recognize my privilege and that not everyone has access to these modalities. This is why I have included the practices at the end of each chapter in this book. These practices are designed to support you in making shifts toward your own transformation, and they are free. A few other free health-supportive, self-soothing techniques to add to your repertoire if you are having a moment of feeling disdain toward your body or yourself include: go outside and walk around the block, lay on the floor and focus on your breath, turn your phone on "do not disturb" for five minutes and sit with yourself, either focusing on your breath or journaling about how you are feeling.

Through this book, I will share with you my knowledge of the physical body, which will include some anatomy. I will also offer practices and tools to support you in getting curious about your own internal and energetic experience through tracking sensations and feelings in your body. The combination of understanding the structural patterns in your body along with understanding your habitual thought patterns will give you the power and resource to finally release anxiety, shame, and self-doubt.

I am giving you the roadmap to guide you along your way through what is not a linear path but one with ups and downs and all the in-between. The more you can find your home within yourself and within your own body, the safer and more resourced you will be to let your light shine brightly and lovingly.

Trauma

We have all experienced varying degrees of trauma, severe experiences that send shockwaves through our psyches and bodies. In response, we have tended to create a pattern of being out of our body. You may or may not relate to this phrasing, but perhaps you've had the sensation of going emotionally numb in a situation that echoes one that was painful for you? Maybe in conflict or in sex you have observed your awareness "leaving" while your physical being stays engaged?

Through this book, I am continuously inviting you into your body. Inevitably, this will bring some uncomfortable emotions and sensations. If you have a history of trauma (maybe you have dealt with sexual assault, abuse, domestic violence, etc.) and don't have much experience with embodiment work, I strongly encourage you to work with a therapist or qualified practitioner as you open these pockets in the body. Some of the sensations may feel jarring and overwhelming. Having someone with whom you can receive one-on-one support is an essential part of the healing process when there is a history of unresolved trauma. Being open to the practices I offer in this book is brave work. I want to make sure you have the support you need to feel and heal deep wounds.

PRACTICE

Five Minutes of Body Time

First, let's celebrate you making the commitment to yourself of beginning and ending each day not plugged into your phone but instead plugged into yourself. Sound the internal applause please. And, if you haven't followed through with that commitment yet, now's your chance.

Spend at least five minutes each day (it can be in your morning or evening quiet time or in the middle of your day) connecting with your body and doing your own internal scan.

If you hate, strongly dislike, or even mildly aren't into your body, it makes sense that it is not a place you spend much time in. It makes sense that it is easier to ignore your body's true wants and override them with what your smart and strong intellect wants. You need to begin allowing yourself more time to simply *be* and do so with the intention of being curious of what the heck is going on in your body.

Close your eyes, breathe deeply but easily, and explore your bodily feelings. Don't *try* to feel anything. Simply let your attention flow through your body. Notice if any feelings of higher or lower vibrations[1] are present in the various parts of your body. Can you, for

1 As human beings, we have access to a large scale and variety of emotions. Some are higher on the scale: joy, contentment, and love. Others are lower on the scale: sadness, anger, and loneliness. Instead of labeling these emotions as negative or positive, which can lead us to judge ourselves or others when we experience certain emotions, I label them as higher and lower vibration emotions. Higher means that when we feel that emotion, it feels good and we perhaps feel more energized or enlivened. Lower means that when we feel that emotion, we feel lower in energy

example, feel your legs? Your feet? Your stomach? Your heart? Notice which parts of your body feel alive with sensation, full, strong, spacious, and/or vital, and which parts seem dull, heavy, lifeless, dimmed, tight, or painful.

During these five minutes, notice how often your attention leaves your body and wanders into daydreams. Does it strike you as odd that it might be difficult to stay in your body for five minutes? If you're not in your body, where are you?

---

and maybe even constricted in the body. I will often refer to thoughts as positive or negative. This is because we have control over our thoughts. Throughout this book, I will use the terms *positive* and *negative* to denote thinking that serves us or works against our well-being.

CHAPTER 3

Identify Your Limitations

The story you tell yourself is the story you will see created throughout your day and throughout your life.

The more you repeat a phrase in your mind, the more your brain begins to believe it is true. Some of these repeated notions may be beliefs that keep you stuck. The first step to creating any sort of change is awareness. Notice what phrases you are repeating. When you are aware of your main limiting beliefs, you will increase your ability to spot them when they come up. Thoughts such as "I can't ever do anything right" hold you back from reaching your full potential. The more awareness you have, the more you will be able to catch your negative thoughts before they spiral out of control and influence your behavior. You can learn how to acknowledge a troubling thought and then see how you can shift it into a more empowering and uplifting one. Productive thoughts don't need to be extremely cheerful but should be realistic. A more balanced thought might be, "I have some weaknesses, but I also have plenty of strengths."

Your conscious mind is your awareness now in the present moment. You are aware of something on the outside as well as some specific mental functions happening on the inside. For example, you are aware of your environment, your breathing, or the chair that you are sitting on.

Your subconscious beliefs are your main driver. Your subconscious mind resembles a fertile garden. If you are not planting seeds to cultivate a desirable crop, weeds (negative thoughts) will grow in abundance. It is *essential* that you are aware of and notice what limiting belief patterns you have. If you don't, you will continue to create more of the low-vibration, self-perpetuating philosophy.

For example, if you believe you don't belong even if you are not consciously thinking that, if it is in the seeds of your subconscious mind, you will be given countless examples of how, yes, you don't belong. You will see evidence of how you don't belong in a group you are a part of, how you don't belong in your neighborhood, etc. Whatever it is, limiting beliefs are the weeds in the garden of our minds. If we do not purposefully uproot them, they will take over until all we see in our daily lives is evidence that they are true.

In Chapters Four to Ten, I will walk you through the ways your own destructive thoughts are limiting you and keeping you stuck.

Rewiring Old Beliefs

Autosuggestion is powerful: the more you repeat something, the more you will believe it. So, let's rewire those outdated limiting beliefs and start replacing them with beliefs that *are true*, reinforcing the seeds that will grow beautiful flowers. I think of this as "healthy self-induced brainwashing." You are feeding your mind thoughts of a creative nature instead of a harmful one. If you neglect your subconscious mind, you can bet those weeds are gonna get out of hand and you will be ensnared by thoughts of a destructive nature.

The key to creating long-term, sustainable change is integrating your mind and body. You must weave these new beliefs and thought patterns through your brain, then down through your nerves and into your body. Ultimately, what I am talking about here is rewiring your nervous system.

Your nerves are wired to send messages to your brain. The longer you have been experiencing a habitual behavior or limiting thought, the deeper that neural groove will be. Think of the Grand Canyon compared to the creek in your neighborhood. The Grand Canyon is a *large* groove. That groove has been etched continuously and with lots of oomph over time. The other, your neighborhood creek, is much narrower; the flow is not as strong. Its groove is not as wide or deep. Water will more readily and easily flow through the grooves of the Grand Canyon than in the significantly smaller grooves of your neighborhood creek.

Use this analogy to give yourself patience through your growth process and to motivate you to continue to heighten your awareness around habitual behaviors and thoughts. When you are tired, highly triggered, sick, or stressed, or when you feel you are at the limit of your emotional capacity, you will more naturally gravitate to your Grand Canyon modes of existence. They require less energy and effort. And that's okay. But notice when this happens. When you notice, you can create a pattern interrupt and make a different choice. Don't allow yourself to get carried so far downstream that you feel as if you are drowning.

You are innovating new ways of being within yourself. Keep practicing. The more you notice and disrupt old ways of being, the deeper the new grooves are becoming. In time, it will become easier for you to choose new modes instead of the larger outdated grooves that limit you.

For each limiting belief, I will share its reverse, the affirmation to disempower it. You will be given a few options for each affirmation.

These affirmations are the desirable seeds you want to plant in your subconscious mind. I suggest that you take these affirmations with you throughout your day, repeating to yourself as you brush your teeth, go on a walk, and after a moment where you found yourself scrolling on your phone for too long lost in mindless comparison land.

The body must also be on board. The mind and body are connected. Plain and simple. You can't affect one without affecting the other. You can accelerate your progress by bringing the affirmations into your physical body. Bringing the new belief and integrating it into your body, so it resonates on all levels with you, is key. You must really feel the vibration of the words you are saying and believe them (at least a little bit) in your bones. As you move through this book, I will guide you through how to do that.

Be *Gentle* with Yourself

Let me say that again; be *gentle* with yourself.

I don't know why, but it feels counterintuitive. I should be harsh and rigid on myself, so I get my act together, right?

When most of us try to change a habit or behavior, our tendency is to be hard on ourselves, to be restrictive and controlling. We have been conditioned to this response to believe that because of our lack of willpower and discipline, we can't create lasting results. So, we become even harder on ourselves, the negative self-talk continues, the old wound of how we are inherently wrong gets activated. The reality is being hard on yourself inevitably leads to more disordered behavior. This is an outdated mode that is hardwired in us from our culture.

The more restrictions I place on myself or are placed on me, the more I swing to excess. Maybe I've had "subtle" thoughts around needing to be more restrictive, or maybe I have cleverly disguised these restrictions as ways of eating to boost my immunity, reduce inflammation, or have a spring cleanse, but it doesn't stick. Sure, maybe it does for a short time but never continuously.

Trying to override your eating habits never works. Trying to work out more to be happier about your body never works. Though clean nutrition and exercise can boost you into more positive thinking, you need to get to the root of what is causing you to be unhappy with your body. What is behind the thoughts of disdain?

Let's also take the labels of "good" and "bad" off food. It's important to be clear for yourself which foods make you feel better and which foods don't leave you feeling so great, but there is nothing inherently "bad" about a food. Putting those sorts of labels on what you eat is giving your power away. So, instead of saying "Oreos are bad," I encourage you to go deeper, asking yourself why you think they are bad? What are you afraid of? What scenarios in the past have supported this labeling of bad?

Bring the power back to yourself, back to your internal experience. Uncover the truth around why you think a food is bad or good. The effort you put into increasing your awareness will support you in moving through outdated beliefs, experiencing more freedom around food, and bringing more love and compassion back to *you.*

I want you to be gentle with yourself not only around food but in a broader sense. If you have a knee-jerk reaction and say something hurtful to your lover or a friend, don't harp yourself about it. If you are moving toward a goal or have a to-do list that you don't quite stick to, be gentle with yourself. When you are gentle with yourself, it gives you the space to pause for a moment instead of getting stuck down the rapid path of resistance and habituation. Being gentle invites in more curiosity, more permission, more opportunity to uncover what is underneath the surface and really vying for your attention. This will support you in making the next forward step to help make things right.

Being gentle with ourselves is foreign to many of us and has been defined repeatedly as weakness. But truly, gentleness is a strength and is forward movement. Taking the gentle approach with yourself regarding your thoughts and actions is a sign of love and progress. Being harsh, rigid, and demanding is not; that is the outdated paradigm that only leads to continual feelings of being stuck and like you are back-sliding.

The Seven Main Beliefs that Keep You Stuck in Body Hate

In my work, I see seven common limiting beliefs time and time again that keep clients stuck in the vicious cycle of displeasure with their bodies. These beliefs are also the ones that dominated my own internal dialogue on my journey toward loving my body. It is important to bring awareness to these limiting belief patterns. When you do, you gain the ability to notice when negative thoughts show up, which in turn gives you the power to interrupt the process and choose a different thought or behavior.

In Chapters Four to Ten, I will take you through each of the seven limiting beliefs, how they impacted my life, how to identify them in your own life, and how to release them. There are guided practices at the end of each chapter. I recommend that you record yourself reading the practices out loud from your phone so that you can then listen to your recordings and really dive into the practices. You can also download the recording for the practice from Chapter Seven on my website at www.wishallwellness.com/radical-embodiment-free-gift.

The following is a brief introduction to these core limiting beliefs about your body that may be keeping you stuck.

I am too fat.

Most of my clients feel they will never be happy or have what they desire until they are a certain size or weight. Almost every single woman I have worked with has felt the need to suck in her stomach in an effort of trying to appear smaller to the external world in the hopes of receiving more approval.

Chapter Four dives deeper into the limiting belief of "I am too fat." In that chapter, you will be invited to consider whether you hold a similar limiting belief and will have the opportunity to create an affirmation as well as a physical body practice to help you move through it.

I am weak.

Too many of us tend to exercise from a place of punishment and should instead do so from a place of pleasure and enjoyment. What happened to the joy of movement? Chapter Five will give you insight into your underlying motivation for movement and exercise and will support you in shifting your focus around movement from a place of harsh self-control to a place of celebration.

I am not enough.

When your focus is primarily on the external world, trapped in comparison with others and sure you are failing, you will subconsciously do everything in your effort to fill that perceived void. You may find yourself lost in constant busy-ness, food abuse, TV, alcohol, shopping, gossip, etc., keeping your mind preoccupied with everything else so you don't have to sit in the discomfort of not feeling enough. In Chapter Six, you will learn a foundational embodiment practice to uncover your enoughness from the inside out.

I am fake.

If you feel unhappy in your body, if you feel too fat, too thin, or too dumpy, your ego may override and try to "posture" (chest up, shoulders back and down, belly in) through it. You want to be seen as "put together," as if you know what you are doing, and so, you posture and project your way through it. Or perhaps you trend toward the opposite, slouching and hiding in your body, curling in to become smaller.

The reality is this posturing is unsustainable and will result in excess tension and pain, as will slumping forward. In Chapter Seven, you will learn a bit about your anatomy. You'll experience a practice to help you find your inherent strength and authentic expression through your body, enabling you to experience more ease, confidence, and integrity.

I am wrong.

Most of us women have been made to feel wrong for the shape of our body. We are also often made to feel wrong for what we crave, whether we seek more food, more attention, more money, more sex, more success, more.

If you have ever squashed your appetite, for food or for life, because you felt ashamed and wrong to admit what you really wanted, you are squashing your deeper yearnings. You are suppressing your appetite for a full and voluptuous life. In Chapter Eight, you will learn how to discern what your cravings are really telling you. You will discover how to peel away the layers of "should" so you know what it is you really desire.

I am too much.

I see this belief *all* too often in the clients I work with. Women have been told their emotions and needs are overwhelming. We try to become smaller because restricting ourselves is what our society promotes.

Chapter Nine will support you in reclaiming those parts of yourself that you have tried—to gain external approval, validation, and success—to make smaller. You get to be too much! It is a part of who you are and often, what you are trying to hold in and make smaller is part of your greater gift to the world. Stop holding back and sucking in and allow yourself to take up space.

I am not worthy.

Advertising is designed to make you feel unworthy. An imaginary "ideal" body is created through digital manipulation, and if your body does not resemble that image, you are made to doubt your value. It's a set-up. You are being seduced to buy so you can fix the broken parts of yourself. But if you give over your power to something external, you will lose yourself.

The practice in Chapter Ten will support you in coming back to yourself and reclaiming your wholeness. It brings together the practices from the book thus far to support you in not only knowing you are worthy on an intellectual level but also in getting to experience your worthiness from a deep cellular level.

Moving Through This Book

As you finish each chapter of this book, I encourage you to record yourself reading aloud the steps for each practice. You can easily do this by using the voice memo on your phone. This way, you can really dive into the practice by listening to it and following along rather than trying to read a step, feel it, read the next, and so on.

I also highly encourage you to try these practices around other people. First, go through the steps solo in a quiet space. Then, once you have a grasp of how the practice is intending to support you within your own body, repeat those steps when you are out and about in public and when you are connecting with others. The real transformation happens when you see changes in your interactions with the world.

Each time you approach a practice from this book, pay attention to how you feel before and after you engage in it. Compare and contrast how you felt before the practice to how you felt after. What do you notice? Name this for yourself. What bodily sensations are present? What thoughts are running or not running through your mind?

Why do this?

I am a *huge* fan of comparing and contrasting how you feel after different practices, movements, meditations, etc. Notice how you felt before your five-minute body scan versus after. What feels different, if anything at all, in your body, your mind, and your spirit? You may receive a clear answer, or instead, you may experience a difference of sensations that is difficult to put words to, but you have a definite distinction in your own body of what feels different.

Acknowledging to yourself what feels different will support you in becoming increasingly able to notice when you start to slip into unhealthy patterns. This is that awareness piece that I was talking about earlier. You will have heightened awareness and will not need the large pain signals (physical pain, anxiety, compulsive overeating, the self-doubt loop, and more unfun experiences) to recognize it is time to reflect and go within.

The more attuned your own awareness is, the quicker you'll be able to bring your power back and make a different choice. Maybe you will choose to sit in meditation, journal, do one of the practices you learn from this book, or move and stretch. Giving yourself the space to look through the before-and-after lens will keep you motivated to utilize nourishing practices that support you in loving your body.

The limiting beliefs listed above are insecurities that plague many of us as women. If you let them grow wild, you will continue to see more of that same story in your reality. They will cloud your judgment and perception. You may think others are judging you for your projected flaw. Often, the judgment you are projecting onto people is not at all what they are thinking. And, as you release these limiting beliefs, when you weed them out of the garden of your mind, you will free up so much space.

Why does this seven-step process work? Because it gives the reins of your well-being back to their proper ownership, *you*. In this process, you won't be bypassing anything. It's going to get uncomfortable. But you will be able to more freely and fully express yourself and begin to love your body a little more.

PRACTICE

Shifting Limitations into Liberations

Carry a journal around for a few days. Capture all negative thoughts. Examples of some negative thoughts: "I'm too fat." "I'm not enough." "I'm stupid." "I don't know enough."

After tracking these thoughts for a few days, look at the list and notice which ones are similar. Circle thoughts that have a similar theme. Then look at your list and identify your main themes of limiting thoughts. What limiting beliefs did you uncover around your body? Looking at those, I want you to identify your main limiting belief/s. What one or two main themes did you identify from your list?

From there, you are going to shift your main limiting beliefs into positive affirmations. As you work through this book, you can shift around your phrases, but for now, pick one affirmation and work with it for at least the next week.

Start with a single affirmation and choose one with which you strongly resonate. The reason I want you to start with one is to help you in really focusing on it, to not feel overwhelmed with remembering multiple phrases, but instead to have one solid affirmation that excites you and that you can rely upon quickly in the moment when you notice your limiting beliefs come up. You can add affirmations as you move forward with this process. I will share a few positive affirmations here to give you some starters to work with. You are welcome to change the words to make it more specific and meaningful to you. Which affirmations (either examples below or ones you created on your own) feel most exciting to you? I want you to pick the phrase that feels the most desirable and tangible in this moment.

- I am strong, resilient, and adaptable.
- I am secure.
- I am confident.
- I am a perfect weight.
- I am beautiful in my body.
- I am the perfect size.
- I am doing the best I can.

When you wake up in the morning, enjoy your first few breaths. Then do your five minutes of checking in with your body, noticing how it feels and what is present. After your body check-in, read your affirmation to yourself.

While you are reading your affirmation, I want you to play with the idea of feeling the words resonate in your body. Don't mentally list them but really allow yourself to feel and enjoy the vibration of your words. Repeat your affirmation out loud a few times to yourself and a few times internally.

As you move through this book, I invite you to continue to track and list your negative thoughts and beliefs. From there, you can continue to add to your affirmations list, which I encourage you to do.

CHAPTER 4

Step One

Permission to Breathe

Limiting Belief: I Am Too fat

Do you hear this thought in your head? Or maybe it's that your thighs are too fat? Or your belly is too fat? Or maybe some version of "I'm not skinny enough," "My belly sticks out," or "I hate how I look in my clothes."

How frequently does this belief come into your head?

Growing up, my family used to go on a canoe trip each summer with my dad's extended family. All day on a canoe. Joyful, right? For me, it was more panic inducing as I would be in my bathing suit all day in front of other people. I was somewhere around the age of ten and as much as I looked forward to this day, I also felt stressed in the days leading up to it. I tried to eat less and went on some sort of undetected diet, hoping my stomach wouldn't look so big.

Sitting in the canoe was a whole other story. Sure, I could have my shirt on over my bathing suit, but there was a lot of jumping in and out of the water so that would get annoying. And, more importantly, I loved (and still to this day love) the feeling of the sun on my skin. But sitting in a bathing suit? That would mean my stomach rolls would be out for all to see. The thought of my own family seeing my belly in broad daylight was humiliating.

I discovered if I sat with a perfectly erect spine, if I tensed all the muscles of my back while sucking in my stomach and pulling my shoulders back, I could diminish the number of rolls. I could make it look like I wasn't so fat. Success!

All day long, I purposefully sat rigid and upright. At some point my uncle, who was in the canoe next to me, commented, "Wow, Emily, your posture is amazing!'

His well-intended compliment embarrassed me. I made up some reason as to why I was sitting so properly and wished the attention away. I desperately hoped no one else would notice how erect I was sitting. I didn't want anyone to recognize that this way of sitting was a newly learned pattern to help me appear smaller. My uncle was genuinely curious and impressed by it. And I did my best to shut down any sort of commentary around it.

I was trying hard to maintain this uprightness. I wasn't doing so to help my spine or overall body alignment. I was doing it because I feared that if my family saw my true stomach rolls, they might reject me. They might think less of me and not be so proud.

Deep down, when my uncle gave me this innocent compliment, I felt the pain of receiving admiration on an action I was doing to reject a part of myself. I pushed that brief blip of pain down and internalized it, never sharing the experience with a soul until a couple decades later.

God forbid I have a stomach. God forbid there be any sort of protrusion showing up from under my clothes in my abdominal region, the space of my body where all my organs are stored, where my uterus, my body's creativity center and resource, resides. Instead of growing up feeling reverence and respect for this space, I tried with all my might to diminish it.

What a waste of energy. Instead of carelessly enjoying a leisurely summer day, with my family out on the canoe, with those who loved me, no matter my shape, all I could focus on was how to sit without looking so fat and walk along the shore without my thighs touching. In lieu of easeful enjoyment, I believed I was fundamentally flawed because I was too fat.

Fat Is Not a Feeling

When I felt fat at the age of eight, what I was really feeling was unacceptable and unlovable. I "felt" fat because of what I witnessed from society, my family, and my peers. I "felt" fat from what I perceived was the acceptable image that a young girl my age should look. Because I didn't see myself as fitting that perceived image, I decided I was unacceptable.

You do not have to be a certain size. This is a stigma. Marketing and advertising are geared to having us feel that being fat is the absolute worst possible thing we could be. If you feel bad, then you will buy more stuff, and the companies selling it will make more money.

In her book, *Happy Fat*, Sofie Hagen, a Danish comedian and co-creator of the Guilty Feminist podcast, writes about the reality of being fat in a world that wants you to take up less space. Fatphobia, Hagen says, is ". . . designed to keep us consuming diet products and miracle foods; and patriarchy—which demands women exert an impossible level of self-discipline around their looks." This system keeps women at war with ourselves, tangled up in pain over our weight and believing it's our fault we are suffering. But each of us has the ability to reject the version of reality we're being sold. At the end of this chapter, I will outline some ways to empower yourself with affirmations, including ways to overcome the limiting belief "I am too fat."

The Good Ol' Sucking in Your Stomach Trick

Sucking in your stomach achieves lots of things, none of which are particularly kind to your body. The action changes the pressure of your abdominal cavity. It creates excess strain on your lower back. It increases rigidity and tension throughout most of your large external muscle groups, which not only takes a massive amount of energy to maintain but is also unsustainable and creates overlaying patterns in your structure that will take years of persistent work to unwind.

When you suck in your stomach, the process significantly restricts your breath. It affects your diaphragm's ability to move up and down as you inhale and exhale. You become unable to access a full deep belly breath. Instead, you rely on shallow breathing through your chest cavity. This causes your nervous system to be in a higher alert setting, aware on a subtle level that danger might be looming. And, yeah, the danger of others seeing your stomach is lurking so you best suck that thing in and suck up the consequences.

Is all this worth it simply to try and appear a couple inches smaller?

Accessing More of Myself

Many years ago, I had a profound experience when I was receiving a Rolf Movement session, a part of Rolfing Structural Integration that focuses on the movement and postural patterns we carry. In the session, we were working with the breath, noticing where my breath went easily and noticing where my breath was more restricted. As the practitioner was slowly moving her hands around my torso, one hand on top and one hand beneath my back, we found my breath's borders.

For the first time ever, I noticed that I could not access my breath in my lower back. My breath was blocked and I couldn't seem to force it there. We worked slowly and gently, going to the spaces in my body where I could bring my breath. After spending some time in those areas, we went to the edges of where I noticed the flow of my breath becoming limited and stopping. We slowly coaxed those parts of my body to relax and ease up a bit.

As soon as I became able to access my breath in my lower back, tears started flowing from my eyes and I began to cry uncontrollably.

The pattern of sucking in my stomach was so strong that when my breath started coming into my lower back (which in order to be able to access meant I couldn't suck in my stomach), my nervous system didn't know what to do. I started shaking and the tears didn't stop. I was experiencing a *huge* emotional release, which felt scary, particularly because it was outside of my voluntary control. My body and nervous system were ready to let go of this old pattern and story of holding, to move beyond it to experiencing more freedom and ease, but my mind was not. So, I shut it down.

I excused myself to use the restroom. Protected by those bathroom walls, I let myself cry but only for a couple minutes. And then I moved on. I splashed cold water on my face and carried through; I was "fine."

On my drive home, it felt as if a spell had come over me. I had an immediate impulse to make a pitstop at the store to load up on food.

Driven by compulsion, I rushed home so I could devour it alone. I felt I had zero control over this behavior.

When my breath came into my lower back, years of suppressed emotions were awakened. My body was ready to release and move on, but my mind wasn't. It didn't feel ready or safe enough to give up my projected mode of being "put together." And thus, I halted this release.

Because I pushed down and suppressed my strong emotional response, as I had for years (in smaller ways) pushed down and sucked in my emotions and feelings, my body went into a strong "cover-up" response so that I wouldn't have to feel the pain. The compulsive overeating was my body's trick of coaxing me out of the hurt, discomfort, and loneliness that my breath had brushed up against. I wasn't conscious of any of this then, but that is when my binge overeating pattern lit up in full force, stronger than it had ever been.

Because I felt too fat for most of my life, I subconsciously restricted each breath. Aside from sucking in my stomach, I can remember countless times where I didn't want to breathe fully as that would expand my torso out, which was the opposite of what I wanted to do. I didn't allow myself full breaths. I would try to breathe smaller and more daintily, so I took up less space. I wanted to cave in on myself and become smaller, smaller, and smaller.

As my breath began to access my lower back, I was touching suppressed and stuck emotions that had been trapped for years. For the first time in a long time, most likely since I was that uninhibited, free, connected little girl on her swing set, I was accessing more of myself.

Emotions and the Breath

There is a direct connection between accessing your breath and feeling all emotions. If your breath is limited, your emotions do not move through you. They become stuck, first resulting in excess tension. With time, this will lead to pain, anxiety, and general feelings of despondency. You will have more rigidity in your body, so there will be less space for experiences and feelings to move through you. You will lose some of your ability to process emotions. You will become more reactive.

When your breath isn't coming down into your belly, you are not connecting to a large amount of your body's capacity. You remain stuck in story, stuck in blame, and stuck in habitual patterns of avoidance, numbing, overeating, complaining, and victimhood. When the breath can move more freely through your body, when you have the capacity to allow your breath to touch its full spectrum, you in turn will be more able to experience and move through the full spectrum of human emotions

Working with the breath is a key focus with every single one of my clients. Initially, most cannot access their breath in their lower back, nor have they ever even been aware of their limitation there. As I guide them in noticing the boundaries of their breath and they gain awareness of where their breathing has been blocked. Often, tears of release follow. When their breath gently nudges up against its edges, restrictions slowly begin to soften. Emotions can flow again more freely. Old memories can be processed and moved through.

The breath can be so meaningful. And the breath can seem so meaningless since we breathe every waking second. But your breath is your lifeline. When you bring your attention to the breath, you are brought back to the present moment. Increasing your consciousness of your breath will allow you to feel grounded and connected, and you will feel more capable of processing the challenges of life.

The Pain of "Good" Posture

Now, let's talk about this "good" posture thing. Often, when I tell people I am a Certified Rolfer, if they have any sort of reference of what Rolfing Structural Integration is, they automatically want to fix their posture by pushing themselves into a rigid, upright posture, forcing their shoulders back and chest up. Though, yes, I love the heightened awareness in these moments that these folks are bringing to their body, I'd love to stop this trend. I'd love for people's responses to instead be one of ease. It would be wonderful to see them check in internally with their body and relax back and down instead of forcing their body into the standard armored position of "good" posture. I would be excited to see them first invite in a deeper exhale, supporting themselves in releasing any excess tension, and then surrender into the support of the ground beneath them rather than fight and strain against gravity.

To help you discover in your own body how to find this more easeful posture, I'm going to start here with a bit of information on breathing and then share detailed steps on how to sit with ease, so get ready for a little anatomy education, my friends. If you already know this information, don't skip over it. Read it with fresh eyes and a new curiosity. Absorb it in a way that supports you in loving your experience in your body a little bit more.

Research shows that having a more erect spine and an open rib cage correlates with having a more positive perception of ourselves.

When we have an upright posture, it automatically supports us in feeling more confident and certain of ourselves. So yes, let's move and sit in healthful upright aligned postures, but not that "good" posture that creates overlaying patterns of tension, pain, and fatigue.

When you breathe better, your posture naturally improves, which in turn allows for more graceful movement. You will begin to feel more fluid. When you allow in those deep, full belly breaths, you elevate your rib cage, which enables it to be in a better position to support your shoulders, neck, and head. With time, this will help to reduce shoulder tension as your shoulders can relax upon the support of your rib cage. This reduction of tension will allow your arms to move more feely as you walk, which in turn helps to generate freer hip and leg movement. A win, win, win, win, win.

Have I convinced you yet to stop sucking in that beautiful belly of yours?

Allowing and giving yourself permission for those wondrous, full, deep abdominal breaths is the perfect first step toward accepting and loving your body a little bit more. Instead of concaving in and becoming rigid, you get to expand out and experience more ease, which in turn helps to expand your perception and the possibilities you see in life.

How to Sit with Natural Alignment

It might seem strange that you are only a few chapters into a book about not hating your body and I'm sharing about how to sit. But this is huge. You must know your basic anatomy and a bit about your pelvis, which is a pivotal part of your overall structural integrity. When you understand your basic structural make-up, you will have a better grasp of how to stack your bones as you sit and stand, so that the rest of your body can relax and soften. Learning to find the support of aligned bones is the key to easy, relaxed posture that does not require the effort of straining, struggling muscles to pull you up or hold you together.

Changing your habits is ultimately an "inside job" that can never be accomplished for you by anyone else. As I have mentioned previously, when it comes to changing any sort of limiting pattern or habit, awareness is key. Cultivating awareness is a challenge for anyone, at any age, but it's worth the effort. I am about to share a detailed description for how to sit with ease, so bear with some detailed steps for a bit.

The following instructions will educate you on how to sit with natural alignment so you can experience more ease and space in your body right away. Start with one point per day. Stick with it for a few days until you feel you have a real comprehension of it in your mind and a feel for it in your body. Notice the sensation of contrast or what is different in your body over time. This is key in creating long-term shifts that will allow you to observe when something feels "off" and recognize what subtle adjustments you can make to veer your ship (your body) in the direction of growth and progress.

1. *Bring awareness to your pelvis and connect to your pelvic bowl.*

    i. The arrangement of the pelvis is the foundation for easy upright sitting. The position of the pelvis determines the angle of the platform on which the spine sits.

ii. Your knees should be lower than your hips.

iii. This allows your pelvis to be tipped forward. One way to remember this is to imagine the pelvis as a bowl of water. In this position, all the water would be poured out the front of the bowl.

iv. Most chairs cause a "sinking" back where your knees become higher than your pelvis. This causes your tailbone (coccyx) and sacrum to be tucked under, which disrupts the angle of the sacral platform on which the spine sits, causing the spine to collapse and become round. This positioning equals you not feeling awesome in your body.

v. Find your sit bones, aka ischial tuberosities (the bones under your butt). Slowly rock your pelvis forward and back to feel the front and back edges of your sit bones.

vi. Now, come to what feels like somewhere between the front and the middle of the sit bones. You will want to be slightly more toward the front.

vii. Let your weight drop down onto the front of your pelvis or pubic bone. From there, imagine a string gently pulling you up from the inside. Imagine that string as a plumb line going down the center of your body, your vertical axis, and let your body relax and soften around that line.

2. *Let your belly be relaxed and see if you can feel your breath in your lower back.*

    i. Relax your belly to allow for a deeper, more relaxed breath. This contributes to your body being in a state that promotes healing.

    ii. Bring your breath to your lower back to release any unnecessary tension that you hold there.

    iii. If you aren't able to feel your breath in your lower back, bring your hand to this area. The external touch from your hand will help you access your breath there. If you find yourself having difficulty experiencing the breath here, give yourself some patience. Start to track where in your back you can feel your breath, and little by little, move your breath lower. This is a process, and I invite you to enter it with gentle curiosity.

3. *Get support from your feet and build an awareness of the front of your spine.*

    i. Your feet provide you with important information on your environment. They help you to orient in gravity, as well as help to gain stability from the ground up while sitting. As you are sitting, feel the floor coming to meet your feet. Feel it supporting you. Bring your focus there.

    ii. Gently press your feet into the ground with a subtle reaching-forward push. When you do this, can you feel the inner line of your legs activate up into your core? If so, take this awareness piece a step further and imagine you can connect with the front of your spine from your feet.

iii. When you think of your spine, you most likely think about your back or the back of your spine. Your spine, particularly your lumbar vertebrae (lower back), go deep inside of you. Having a reference and awareness of the front of your spine is one of the most important steps in being able to find your own inherent strength while feeling vulnerable, open, and soft. We will talk more about this in Chapter Seven. For now, begin to be curious about this space and create a connection to it.

iv. See if you can allow your belly to be relaxed from here.

If you would like a printed copy, you can download and print out the above "How to Sit with Natural Alignment" practice by going to www.wishallwellness.com/radical-embodiment-free-gift. Place the instructions on your desk or somewhere you will see them every day when you are sitting. Take one bullet per week and keep it at the forefront of your mind, strengthening your awareness muscles and mastering each step.

PRACTICE

Expanding Your Breath

I have shared what it can be like to experience your breath in your lower back and to increase the fullness of your breath. Now, I'd like you to experience what that feels like in your body.

Lay on the ground, knees bent. Start by gently noticing your breath. As you go through this practice, I don't want you to force anything. Don't effort too hard to feel something. Keep a state of gentle curiosity. And please, don't let my experience persuade you into thinking you are doing this wrong. This goes for all of the practices in this book. We are each in our own individual bodies. I *invite* you to notice what is going on for you and your body.

As you are laying and breathing, feel the rise and fall of your belly. Feel it inflate with each inhale. Feel it deflate with each exhale. As you inhale, can you also feel your ribs elevate and expand? Your rib cage works like an accordion when you breathe, and ideally it moves in three directions. When you breathe in, the front of your rib cage expands as it elevates forward and up, the sides of your rib cage expand out, and the back of your rib cage also expands out. With each inhale, you have the potential to gain space in three directions through your rib cage.

Most of us tend to only breathe through the front of our bodies. Start with noticing your breath there. Then bring your attention to the sides of your rib cage. Are you able to feel those expand up and out with each inhale? If not, bring your hands just underneath each armpit, arms crossed as though you are giving yourself a little hug. Use the tactile feedback of your hands to help inform the breath to reach that area.

Now check to see if you can feel your breath expanding back through your rib cage. Can you feel your shoulder blades sliding wider apart as you breath in? Uncross your arms and place your hands under your upper back. If your shoulder range of motion is an issue, place a towel or small blanket under your upper back. See if you can notice your breath filling up your upper back and rib cage. Sit here for a few moments, allowing your breath to dance around, filling up the entire dimensionality of your rib cage.

After enjoying your breath for several minutes, move your hands and/or blanket underneath your lower back. Allow your belly to be soft here. As you move your breath into your lower abdomen, can you also feel your breath coming into your lower back? If not, can you identify how low in your back you can trace your breath going? Do you feel the locations of the edges of your breath? Gently and lovingly bring your breath to those boundaries, inviting in more ease and space to those areas. Be here for as long as you like.

Compare and contrast how you feel internally before doing the practice versus after. Are you more relaxed afterward? Do you feel softer? Are you more present, awake, and aware? What do you notice about your mental and emotional state?

The above is a beautiful practice to do as a part of your daily routine as well as at times when you feel triggered, agitated, or stressed. You can add it to your morning or evening airplane mode, body love time. As you repeat the practice, notice how much easier it becomes to access your breath in different areas, particularly your back. Give yourself patience if you feel you were unable to bring your breath into your back. With time, simply by having the intention to increase your breath capacity and heighten your awareness, your breath will naturally take up more space.

So, are you too fat? Or has that concept been impressed on you by an industry and a society that depends on your self-hatred? How about taking that limiting belief and flipping it around?

- I am exactly the right weight.
- I deserve to take up space.
- I embrace my shape and size.

Work with an affirmation that celebrates your size as you go through your day. Tape it to your closet door. Hum it in the shower. The opposite of oppression is freedom, and you have a right to feel the glory of your *exactly right* body, in all its lumps and smoothness, in all its muscles and curves, and in the glory of its uniqueness.

As you work with these practices, you may also want to integrate the affirmation that you came up with from the practice at the end of Chapter Three. With the How to Sit practice, when you allow your belly to expand fully with your inhales, repeat your affirmation. As you do the Expanding Your Breath practice, repeat your affirmation. Integrate your affirmation with other feel-good body things you are already doing and say it to yourself when you notice limiting thoughts coming in to create a pattern interrupt.

CHAPTER 5

Step Two Move from Within

Limiting Belief: I Am Weak

Has this thought lurked in your mind regarding moving, not moving, and life? With the gym, do you feel weak about your self-discipline because you don't go as consistently as the others there or because you're not quite as strong as you used to be? Do you even go to the gym? You must be a weak person if you can't get your act together and freaking make your workout.

When you believe you are weak, physically or mentally, you are giving some of your power away. What you focus on amplifies. Physically, yes, maybe it is true; you are weaker in some muscle groups of your body than in previous times in your life. The acknowledgment of that could support you in wanting to do something different, like initiating consistent strength training, and that is great. But don't keep your attention on how you are weak. Awareness with this habit, as with other aspects of the body love journey, is key. And from it can come meaningful change.

Notice your thoughts that depict you as weak. Maybe you are doing a shoulder press or push-ups and recognize you used to be able to achieve more. Instead of getting sucked into the thought pattern of

"I am so weak," you have another option. Cut a new neural pathway by reminding yourself how powerful you are beginning to feel *right now*. Observe how much more energy you get from the positive reframing.

If "I am weak" shows up more for you in how you perceive yourself mentally and if you see yourself as weak because you can't push yourself out of bed, get out the door to the gym, or finish that project, bring your awareness to it. Ask yourself why you feel this way. Ask whose words or actions are making you feel weak. Approach your self-assessment with curiosity instead of trying to override your mind and shove it away.

When you push an aspect of yourself away, it doesn't wander off. It only comes closer. If you attempt to force a thought or judgment out of your mind, it will continue to sit in your subconscious, becoming like a noxious weed that you just can't seem to get rid of. Instead of pushing it away, which only deepens its roots, embrace that uncomfortable thought. Hold it in this state of gentle curiosity that I am continuously encouraging. From this space of embracing and acknowledging it, you will have the ability to move through it. You'll be able to figure out where this weed's roots are and take them out.

Movement for Punishment

I'm the youngest of seven kids: three boys and four girls. There's about a decade's difference between me and my oldest sibling. When I was eight years old and had first begun to believe I was "too fat," my older siblings, who were in high school, would occasionally go to the YMCA to work out. I envied this. I desperately wanted to go and grind out calories on the elliptical, to sweat out all my badness and shame. I was convinced the YMCA was the solution to my body woes. The gym didn't even allow someone my age to work out alone, so, I would have to impatiently wait until I was sixteen, the age when I could finally work out solo there.

In junior high, I joined track and discovered that running helped me be skinny. I would carefully pack my lunch, counting out seventeen wheat crackers (the suggested serving size) and one string cheese. I convinced myself this was enough food to fill me up. Some days, I was "successful" and only ate that portioned number of crackers and bit of cheese for lunch. When I did this, I would feel so proud of myself for completing my after-school track workout even though my tummy was rumbling from the start.

I was near the edge of an eating disorder, but my struggle wasn't detectable to the external eye. I restricted my calories. I made sure to run every day, not for the joy of it, but because running was how I was going to stay skinny. I remember people commenting on how my face was thinning out and I was losing my baby fat, an accomplishment indeed.

Once during that time, I was at a friend's house for an overnight sleepover. I had guiltily eaten a couple of cookies. Someone said something that I now can't remember, but I do recall the comment made me feel bad about myself. This amplified the guilt I felt for eating those cookies. I said I needed to go pee. Instead, I went to the bathroom and threw up those cookies. I didn't deserve them. I was bad for having them. They were not to be allowed if I wanted to stay skinny. I went back to the living room to hang with my friends as though nothing had happened. I loathed myself for not having better control of this horrendous problem of my body, mentally noting that I needed to run extra the next day.

In high school, I was finally old enough to go to the YMCA alone. There was a period where I would go at 5:00 a.m. to exercise before school. I would eat only one granola bar for breakfast. I was rigidly counting my calories, trying so hard to keep my body maintained to an appropriate size that was sure to be approved of and would receive nods and kind words from others.

Let's get rid of this cultural obsession with working out to punish ourselves for eating and to burn off calories. Yes, sometimes a good sweat session on the StairMaster blasting out to your favorite tunes is the perfect therapy for you. But be aware of the why behind what you are doing.

Are you exerting yourself to look smaller or to gain the approval of others? Do you start a new movement challenge because you feel guilty and feel the need to chastise your body for the times you overate? Do you exercise only to dominate your body? Ask yourself if you are creating exercise goals as a form of punishment because you believe there is something wrong with your body rather than exercising to celebrate what your body can do.

Even if you think you are well-intentioned with your underlying goals for movement, I encourage you to look closely here. I want you to move. But not from a place of, yet again, another "should." Instead, move for the sheer delight it gives your body.

Tune into your motivation before each movement session. Keep connecting and anchoring back into the celebration of what your body can do and how you want to feel. If you notice you are wanting to exercise because you feel too fat, too weak, or the like, observe the thoughts. No need to judge yourself here. We are all human and these thoughts may come. You get to step into your power when you recognize these thoughts, acknowledge them, create a pattern interrupt, and choose a different, more empowering thought, perhaps the affirmation you have been working with. Allow that more uplifting thought to be what drives you forward.

When you shift your why for movement and exercise from a "should" because your body is wrong to a "why" based on honoring your body's miraculous capacities, you will more naturally stay consistent with your movement, experience less resistance, and generally feel better. Because you are not being hard on yourself, you get to connect with yourself and enjoy the ways your body can move.

Movement for Pleasure

Movement is a gift. It is a way to honor your body and reward it for being so capable, so strong, so adaptable. Movement can feel *so* pleasurable.

Before my mind became clouded by how I perceived I was supposed to look, I would spend hours as a child frolicking around my yard, swinging, skipping, biking through the neighborhood. This amounted to tons of movement, technically tons of exercise, but all of it was for play and sheer enjoyment.

As a kid, what movements did you love to do? What physical activities now help you feel joyful and free? Dancing, swimming, rolling on the ground? A sauntering walk with your pup? Going upside down against the wall in a handstand and playing with your scary edge? Hula hooping or skating?

Each week, I participate in a Sensually Embodied Dance class based on Sheila Kelley's S-Factor. The overlying intention of the class isn't to dance sexily. Instead, it is to allow your body to move as it wants to move based on what movement feels delicious and sensual. The class is focused to support you in entering your body and noticing which movements, perhaps even the gentle sensation of your breath, feel most pleasurable.

In the class, your body gets to decide how much or how little it wants to move. Your body is what moves *you*, rather than your mind deciding how the body should move. There's plenty of rolling on the floor, slithering around the pole, and pressing up against the wall in this class. I find getting to drop into my body and out of my story to be tremendously therapeutic. When I leave, I feel the release from the tension that has melted away from my body. I experience much more space and ease, in my body and my thoughts.

When you tune into your body and discover how it wants to move, you might be surprised by what comes next. This is so important especially if you identify as female. Give permission for the feminine to express herself through movement. The feminine isn't linear, rigid, or predictable. She requires safe space and patience to come out, unwind, and play.

At least once a week, invite into your life the idea of moving to feel pleasure. First, I want you to know this sensation, particularly in regard to feeling pleasure while you are moving, might be strange, scary, or unfamiliar, and that is okay. Sit quietly with your body and your breath. This alone can be a beautiful way to uncover pleasure once again. Ask your body what movement would feel oh so good. Pay attention to how you can alter your motions, perhaps staying longer in a stretch or performing the slowest bicep curl to feel more pleasure. When you are engaging in physical activity to feel pleasure versus moving to punish your body, the likelihood of you moving every single day and experiencing enhanced vitality, energy, and clarity increases a thousandfold. And the more you choose to move to feel pleasure, the more that feeling of pleasure and enjoyment will ripple out into the rest of your life.

Movement to Shift Perception

When you are mostly sedentary, you see only what is in front of you. Your visual periphery does not change all that much, if at all. The fascia in your body begins to mold and become overly fibrous in the areas that are supporting you in how you are sitting. (See the upcoming section for a discussion on fascia.) Those muscle groups form a collagen matrix overlay that, in time, limits the ability of each muscle group to be able to move independently. Things start operating as a clump. You may experience this in your own body as feeling not only tighter and more restricted but also kind of clunky and not aligned when you walk.

Think about how this impacts the way you think and feel emotionally. If you have a bout of sadness, being physically stuck can make it challenging for you to healthfully process through that emotion. The rigidity created in your body when you are mostly sedentary can make you easily feel overwhelmed and maxed out. Because there is less physical space in your body, you will more readily turn to numbing behaviors of binge watching TV, eating food, or becoming lost in a spiral of negative thoughts and stories.

If a spurt of anger strikes you, you will be more reactive. Think of the tension on a rubber band. If it is stretched to its limit, it won't take much of a pull to make it snap. Similarly, if tensional pulls in your body are near their limit in your tissue, you may feel the tension physically, and you will snap emotionally, whether that be through a hot fury of words to your loved ones, colleagues, pet, or, internally, to yourself.

Movement isn't simply the antidote to being sedentary and thus stuck. It offers its own opportunities for our growth and transformation. Our minds are wired to focus on what is not working. That is where they will automatically go unless we can catch them. Movement is *huge* in helping to rewire your brain. It is a hugely receptive time to send affirmations to your body of how strong, capable, and amazing it is. Feel those words as you push through your heels and conquer the steep incline or stroll down your neighborhood sidewalk.

Linear Movement

Typically, the ways we move are in a linear, frontal plane. We tend to move forward, sometimes backward, and occasionally side to side. We don't tend to twist, spiral, and move in multiple planes, or if we do, it is more of a rarity.

As a Certified Rolfer, the system I am working with in my practice is the fascia. I think of the fascia as your soft tissue skeleton. If you took away almost everything in your body—bones, blood, muscles, organs, etc.—and left only the fascia, you would be left with a spider web-like structure that very much looks like you. The fascia spirals through your body. It connects everything. It is not linear. It is not only in one plane. It has fibrous and elastic properties. You need both. You need the more fibrous areas, the parts that have a stronger collagen matrix, to give your body structural integrity and hold things in place. You need the elasticity to be able to move fluidly and easily. With time, repetitive movement patterns, injuries, and overlaying postural patterns, you become overly fibrous in certain areas and lose the elasticity in your fascia.

If you want to feel free in your mind and body, you must unwind. And as is true with our fascia itself, the unwinding process isn't linear. To shift from "I am weak" or "I am too big" to "I am strong and flexible" and "I am the perfect size for me" and to believe and integrate the new belief through your system on a cellular level, you gotta roll with it. Like, literally, roll on the floor, roll on your mat, roll up against the wall. Rolling is simply one example here, but I am using it as it is a way for you to move your body in a non-linear way, which is essential for the overall well-being of both your tissue and your mindset.

I'm a huge fan of foam rolling. Often, when I suggest foam rolling to clients of mine, a grimace appears on their face. That is because all too often, the type of foam rollers that people use are overly dense. Thus, when you are rolling out on them, it is painful and uncomfortable. Less popular are soft density foam rollers. This gentler approach to foam rolling supports your nervous system in settling instead of going into an agitated stress response from the demand of the hard density rollers. You can surrender into them, taking deep breaths in and out as you are rolling or laying on them, helping your tissue to melt.

This is so good for your body. And it can feel so good. Instead of a grimace when I mention foam rolling or any sort of self-myofascial soft tissue release, I'd love to see a smile of delight and pleasure. You can receive so much pleasure in doing this. It can feel so good. You can release much unnecessary tension that builds up throughout your day as you listen to the news, receive email blasts, have a conflict with someone at work, or rush to that appointment you forgot and are now late for. These small daily stressors that are easy to overlook all add up.

What you choose to do for your own movement practice has a huge impact on the overall health, well-being, and fluidity you get to experience in your body as a whole. Cognitively speaking, something different happens when I do a form of movement that incorporates spirals and rotations than from when I do my typical movement patterns (think running and spinning). When you dance along a pole or roll around on the floor, your fascia moves and unwinds in the twist that it has desired for years. The movement allows tension to release and rigidity to ease up, creating more space and peace, more contentment and resiliency.

The Days You Don't Feel Like Moving

Do it anyway. But don't force yourself through it. Don't yell at yourself to suck it up and push through. Get curious about the why behind your resistance before you just decide to override your body and power through. You don't need to come to a full conclusion, but it is important that you allow a bit of silence so you can listen to yourself.

Then, if you still don't feel like moving but conclude it would serve your greater good, go for a walk. Bring your headphones and listen to your favorite tunes or tune into the sounds of nature or your city. Maybe get on your foam roller and do some gentle foam rolling to bring some movement, more ease, and space into your tissues. Perhaps you decide to simply lie on the ground and notice how much movement you can get through your body from each breath. Starting is normally the most difficult piece. Often, once you start to shift your body just a bit (rolling on the floor, gently stretching, dancing to that song that always gets you going, whatever it may be) you will find that you desire to move even more.

PRACTICE
Feel Good Movement

Earlier, I recommended that you amplify the effects of the affirmation you initially chose to counteract a limiting belief by integrating it into your sitting and breathing practices. Now, I will ask you to take the process a step further by working with an affirmation related to movement. Here are a few to choose from but feel free to create your own or reword one of these so it resonates with you:

- "I am strong and capable."
- "I am moving because if feels sooo good."
- "I am powerful."

As you engage in physical activity this week, be that a walk, an intense workout, or dancing solo in your room, bring your affirmation to mind (the one you have already been working with as well as the new one related to movement). Repeat the affirmation to yourself as you move. Feel the vibration of the words landing into your body, turning you on in a new way.

At least one time each week, gift yourself a session of Feel Good Movement. Block off your desired amount of time, put your phone on do-not-disturb, set your timer, and connect within to see how your body wants to move. Start with your simple body check-in. Notice how you are feeling. Ask your body how it wants to move. This time is for you, so let it be fun and playful, let it feel good. It doesn't have to be another area that you're "doing wrong" or just another "to-do" you are checking off your list.

As you are moving, also play with experiencing the full expansion of your breath. As you walk down the street, can you access your breath through your back? Can you feel that accordion expansion of your rib cage? Your movement time gets to be a juicy welcome home to your body.

CHAPTER 6

Step Three Find Your Enoughness

Limiting Belief: I Am Not Enough

For the majority of my life, I believed I was not enough. Going about my days, my head was full of judgment. I sized up others to help my ego feel a little bit better while simultaneously criticizing myself for all the ways I was insufficient: my body didn't measure up, I was boring, and I wasn't successful enough. I was just lowly me, insecure, and a little depressed. And because of all of that, I believed I was not enough to have the relationships I wanted or put myself out there in my career.

The "I am not enough" belief will rob you from experiencing the delight present in your life now. The pain of it will make you feel like you need to constantly strive. It will hold your mind in a frenzied state of constantly comparing yourself to others. The internal void will have you buying anything that gives the slight promise of "fixing" you. It will make you take care of everyone else, every little to-do, before it even occurs to you to ask yourself, "How do I feel?" and "What do I need?"

If you believe that you will not be enough until you can prove through external factors (body size, income, a house, a car, the "perfect" relationship) that you are enough, you won't experience contentment. If you're operating with this framework, when you are externally validated, your mind will have already moved to the next thing that you must do or get so you can again be enough. Body hate, body dissatisfaction, body loathing, and body dysmorphia are all rooted in the feeling of not being enough. If your body is fat, if your body is in pain, if your body has cellulite or is the wrong shape, whatever it may be for you, the belief of "I am not enough" will continuously have its way with you and drive your ship.

What is your "I am not enough" voice holding you back from?

Womb Space

Several years back, thanks to a business coach I was working with at the time, I met Rachael Jayne Groover. I went to a free talk she was giving, curious to learn more about her, but also mentally set on not having the time or financial resources to commit to any work she might be offering. Everything she was teaching completely resonated with me and I knew it would transform my life. Because I felt like I wasn't ready to invest further, I told myself I would be consistent and practice the tool she gave us on my own. Fortunately, I quickly realized that was not my highest self speaking and knew I needed more accountability and support, and so I signed up for her three-day Art of Feminine Presence Workshop. Attending the weekend felt right and I trusted that feeling.

That weekend shifted the trajectory of my life. Sounds exaggerative and yet it's true. For the first time in my entire life, without effort, without trying to overpower my brain, I felt enough. My mind's old games of comparison and seeing myself or others as less than weren't there. My familiar mode of projecting out that I had it all together vanished.

The reason behind this remarkable shift was learning how to inhabit my womb space. That actual embodied feeling of being in the center of my body allowed me to feel true belonging to my *Self*. I wondered why, in my life-long quest for figuring out how to feel enough, this had never come up, why I had never been taught about my feminine essence.

You have a physical body: your muscles, bones, blood, fascia, etc. And you have an energetic body: the life force or chi that runs through and around you. In all healing, martial arts, and yogic traditions, a key energetic center in the body is the womb space (lower abdomen for men). In Chinese Qigong it is known as the Dantien; the Japanese name is Hara. I will refer to it as the Dantien here as that is most commonly used.

This power center is located in the center core of your body, about three inches below your navel and back toward the spine. The Dantien is considered to be the house of physical communication, sensory awareness, and feelings. When something is going on in your environment or in another person, you can feel that in your own body. Have you ever had a gut feeling about something? That inner knowing comes from this space. These feelings can be subtle at times, perhaps a quiet whisper. The more you pay attention to your Dantien or your womb space, the clearer this communication becomes.

During that weekend, I discovered how to experience the present moment through my physical body and feel my enoughness from the inside out. Even though I had already invested what little money

I had toward business and personal growth programs, I signed up at the end of the workshop for a year-long Feminine Leadership Mastery Program. I knew I needed this. I put down my deposit and with excited confidence, committed myself to a year of diving deep into this work.

The week after the workshop, I was at an Orange Theory class, a fitness class that involves the treadmill, rowing machine, and weights. I had been attending these classes for a couple months and always tried my best to be somewhat invisible. I found the instructor attractive but believed I wasn't possibly fit or skinny enough for him. I usually felt some degree of inadequacy in the class but kept going as I loved the way I felt after the workout and was training for a half marathon.

After discovering how to inhabit my womb space, I noticed a significant shift in how I felt in the class. I felt spunky. I felt attractive even though I was sweating my ass off in an old t-shirt. I felt as if the instructor noticed me more, giving me more smiles and acknowledgment. As I ran on the treadmill, I had a sly smile on my face as I played with sprinting from my womb space. I felt playful and fun. I felt enough. Enough to approach the instructor. Enough to feel like I belonged to this crew of hard work-outers. Enough for whatever it was I desired. Being in your womb space is what will help you know (that deep true embodied knowing that is completely different from knowing intellectually) that you are enough.

Who knew this organ could be so powerful? Okay, so maybe you did, but I sure as hell did not.

Presence

When you are in your womb space, you are home. Presence is being home in your body.

Some people have presence; some people don't. Think of a person walking into a room, and all eyes are on her. Think of another person walking into a room, and no one notices her. The difference in these two people? It's not what they are wearing, whether one has makeup on, or anything to do with what they look like. The difference is one has presence; she is owning her space by *inhabiting* her body. The other one does not; she is popped out of her body, lost in thought.

Your physical presence is the number one thing that attracts people to you and makes them listen to you. We all get in our heads from time to time, particularly in situations where we feel nervous or inadequate. Because of this, we project out into the world a persona or emotional state that is not aligned with our current state of being. We feign that we "have it all together" or are "perfect," or we go to the opposite spectrum of feeling invisible, stuck in our heads and out of our body, convinced we are not good enough. When we perform or dissociate out of comparison or insecurity, we end up feeling exhausted by the end of the day. We become less visible and less magnetic. We lose our potency and power.

But, when we can anchor into our body and not get lost in anxious thought loops, we feel calm, grounded, steady, and *enough*.

Your presence is a gift. Most importantly, it is a gift to yourself.

I Am Enough

Discovering how to embody my womb space was one of my biggest saving graces. In moments when my self-doubt talk is strong or the yearning to engage in a compulsive behavior strikes, as I connect to my womb space, I can slow that train and then make a different choice. Consistently connecting into this space, and within your body in general, helps to rewire your nervous system, reclaiming your body as a safe territory instead of something you avoid at all costs.

The more you invite most of your awareness to reside within your body, the more you will naturally feel that you are enough. Likewise, while holding and moving toward the vision of what you desire and want in life, you *get* to experience your enoughness. No need to wait until you have some elusive magical appeal, cross another "to-do" off your list, or change something about your body. You are enough. Simply as is.

Being aware that you are enough is not an intellectual knowing. It is an actual embodied knowing. There is a distinct difference between the two, so don't fool yourself into thinking, "I got this," when really you haven't experienced it on a cellular level. Without a true bodily understanding, the "I am not enough" belief remains wired strongly through you and continues to be your underlying motivation for why you strive for more.

What gets to be possible when you shift the pattern in your system from illusion of "I am not enough" to the true story of "I am enough"?

When you feel your own fullness (through inhabiting your body), the incessant need to fill the void isn't there. You get to conserve energy because you are not constantly trying to prove yourself. You get to relax back and down within yourself. The following practice will support you in experiencing your enoughness now. It has been the most foundational piece in my own transformation as well as for many of my clients.

PRACTICE

Womb Space[2]

This is a great practice to do while being witnessed by someone else so you can receive immediate feedback on how you are perceived. But for now, try it by yourself and see what you notice.

You will need a voice memo recorder on your phone for this practice. This may seem silly or strange, but I want you to have an actual tangible sense of what you sound like after you complete each of the following practices.

Head Space:

This is where most of us spend most of our time, lost in thought, worry, or fear about what might happen, or fantasizing about what could happen. You are not anchored into your body. You are not in the moment. The voice of "I am not enough" lives here as do the voices of comparison and ego. We are more forgettable when we are in this space because we have less presence, which also results in us not feeling seen or heard.

Think about your to-do list or bank account, something that creates some low-level anxiety for you. From this space, just above your head, talk for thirty seconds to one minute about your day. Anything you want to recall. Record this on your smartphone. Don't worry about what you are going to say; simply start recording and talk from your head space about your day.

---

2 The womb space practice is a practice that Emily learned from Rachael Jayne Groover, creator of the Art of Feminine Presence. Emily went through the Art of Feminine Presence Teacher Training with Mrs. Groover.

Womb Space:

Now, I want to invite you into your body. Sit on a chair with both feet on the ground. Gently close your eyes. Bring your breath into that beautiful belly of yours. Slowly begin to bring your attention to the lower half of your body. Place a hand on your lower abdomen about three inches below your belly button, with your attention back toward your spine, at the center point of your pelvis. Imagine a light or crystal here.

As you breathe, imagine your womb space breathing with you. Allow this energy center to ground and anchor you into the present moment. Staying connected here, again record yourself talking about your day on your voice memo for thirty to sixty seconds. As before, don't worry about the words or what you are going to say. Simply do your best to stay connected to your center while you talk.

Comparison:

First, before you listen to the recordings, write down in your journal what you noticed in each mode. How did you feel speaking from your head space? How did you feel speaking from your womb space? What do you remember saying from each mode?

Now listen to each recording. Does the sound of your voice shift? If so, what changes in the quality and tone of it? Do you use different words or expressions to describe your day? Does what you remember about your day change? Notice how the recordings differ.

The above is a practice I do a lot at the start of my group work with women, pairing participants in twos. It's amazing what a difference each woman notices between these two modes within herself as well as the woman she is witnessing. When a woman speaks from her head space, usually her partner doesn't really remember much of what she said. Typically, the head space shares are focused around the woman listing what she has done, fairly factual and flat. When a woman shares from her womb space, she generally shares more how she was feeling with each item she did during her day. There tends to be more emotion and vulnerability in what she expresses, as well as a sense of gratitude. Her partner not only remembers what she said but also feels more connected to her and curious to learn more.

As with the other practices, introduce an affirmation to replace the limiting belief you may be carrying. How does it feel to become aware of your womb space, feel your energy there, and say the words "I am enough"?

Womb space for those who have had trauma:

Entering your womb space can be complicated if you have experienced sexual trauma. If you can't feel this part of your body, or if attempting to inhabit it shakes loose pain from your past, ask yourself, "What part of my body can I take back today?" Start there. If emotion comes up, that is a good thing. Any tears that may arise are the resistance that's holding you back. Use the analogy of an elevator to support you in moving further down your body, one level at a time. Know that there is no need to rush and honor the fact that accessing this space in yourself can be emotionally intense. If you have experienced sexual trauma in the past and haven't received support from a therapist, I highly recommend finding a therapist to work with to make sure you have the container necessary to process what is ready to be released.

CHAPTER 7

Step Four
Access Your Authentic and Vulnerable Strength

Limiting Belief: I Am Fake

Most of my life, I lived with the belief that to be loved, liked, and accepted, I needed to show up as having it all together. I needed to be perfect and happy.

When someone asked how I was, I would answer with a well-rehearsed smile and respond, "I'm good." Sure, some of the time, I was good. And, yes, I don't need to air my dirty laundry to every person who asks how I am. But even when my family and dear friends checked in on me and truly wanted to know how I was, I responded in this way. I faked being happy even when I wasn't and felt isolated and lonely.

I feared these feelings. I thought they meant something was wrong with me, that I was lacking in some way. So, I put on my good, forced posture that I had practiced since I was a child, I sucked my stomach in, held my shoulders back, and carried myself in an air of false confidence.

Many years ago, I was receiving the Rolfing 10-Series, a process of ten sessions that work through the body in a holistic and transformative way. Halfway through the series, I had a dramatic realization. I was out on a twilight walk through my quiet neighborhood in Boulder. Suddenly, I realized how *easy* it was to walk. I felt as if I was gliding. I checked in with my body to determine where I was in relation to gravity and realized I was perfectly aligned. And I wasn't making an effort! I wasn't trying to hold myself up in my old "good" posture.

An overwhelming amount of emotion came over me. Tears filled my eyes. I realized that all my life I had been pretending through posturing my body to project that I was "good" and "had it all together" to gain others' acceptance.

In that moment, I knew I no longer wanted to pretend. It was exhausting, futile, and ultimately meaningless. In this newfound sense of my body, I was aligned. I felt strong and stable, and at the same time, I felt open and spacious. I felt I had the capacity to be vulnerable and authentic, while still feeling capable and secure. It was the most incredible sensation and discovery. I could simply *be*.

I Am an Imposter Posturing

Hating your body will drive you into wanting to be someone else, anyone but yourself. No thank you to this physical vessel. It just won't do. It is crummy and slow and stupid and lethargic and lazy. If people knew that, they would not want to work with you, date you, or be friends with you. You feel your body is inept and so you must armor it up, posturing your way through, feigning competence and confidence. Or perhaps you collapse, caving in on yourself, shoulders rounded forward with your spine following, losing height and strength, and giving up on all your dreams.

Posturing:

The subconscious pattern of holding your body a certain way to project out into the world a false sense of confidence and togetherness. What is fascinating is how this mode is usually perceived by others. When you project and posture, others usually see you as some combination of arrogant, needy, unfriendly, and unapproachable. This is most likely not the impression you want to give off. Anytime you project a way of being that is incongruent with your emotional state on the inside, it will feel icky to others. They won't be able to put words to it, but they will know they don't quite trust or like you.

Living at Kripalu, the yoga retreat center, was one of the best decisions of my life. It is where I learned that I wasn't the only one with the pestering monkey mind thoughts of "I'm an imposter." Living in that ultra-contained bubble was simultaneously a gift and a source of exhaustion with everyone needing to be so present, authentic, and conscious all the damn time. Once in the dining hall, I was filling up my mug with some hot water. A woman came up from behind me to compliment and exclaim how good my posture was. Oh, how I cringed inside. I felt as though she was calling my bluff. Could she see how hard I was trying? Did she know how far from my body's integrity I was in producing this posturing affect? I felt like a fake.

On a walk recently, I was sharing with a friend how this old limiting belief was nudging its way into my awareness. He graciously shared that if people didn't feel a bit like that while writing a book, then they were probably a sociopath. This gave me a good chuckle and sense of ease through my system.

Being On Versus Being Tuned In

All too often when it comes time for me to show up for work, an event, a date, the initial mode that wants to drive my show is the feeling is one of needing to "be on." I feel as if I need to prove I am valuable enough for the amount I am charging, important enough to be talked to, deserving of a promotion, the list goes on. When that need to prove is in the driver's seat, I posture, trying to be on, a struggle that requires so much energy, is exhausting, and always feels bad.

There is a distinct difference I feel in my entire body and system between "being on" and being "tuned in." When I tune in, I get to just be. No effort is required. When I tune in, there is a softening that happens through my body as I take a deep breath and connect with myself, relaxing into presence.

Discovering my womb space and releasing years of muscular strain were monumental in my ability to tune in more fully instead of trying to "be on." In the walk I described earlier in this chapter, the focus of the Rolfing session I had just received was to help release my psoas muscles (more on these below). That work, without my having any sort of intellectual awareness of it at the time, immediately allowed me to discover my inherent strength and support, which resulted in me feeling open and receptive. When I tune in, I experience life more richly, and I am a better coach, facilitator, and bodyworker. Instead of "being on" for my clients, I get to tune in to what is true and present.

The Muscle of Your Soul

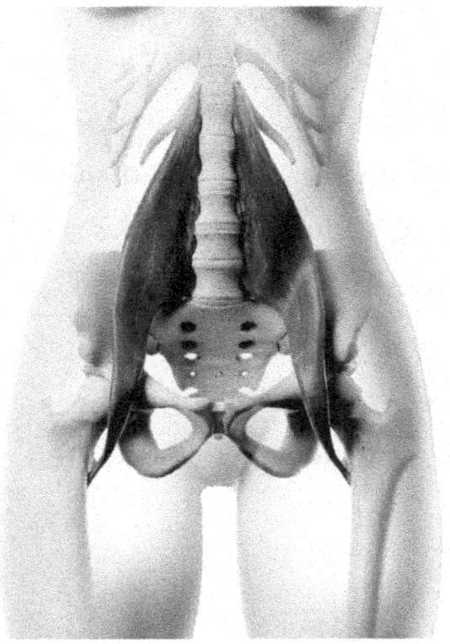

Your psoas muscles are significant contributors to your structural support and foundation. It's important to know the anatomy for what I'm about to share, so bear with me for just a bit. Your psoas muscles are the only muscles that attach your legs into your spine. They are your main hip flexors. The psoas muscles originate from the front of your low spine (lumbar vertebra) and fan down through the back of the pelvis to insert themselves to the inside of your upper thigh (femur). Ideally in movement, particularly in walking, that movement of hip flexion as you walk is initiated from the psoas muscles.

From the time you start school, when you are only about six years old, you are sitting most of your day. Think about the anatomy I just shared. The psoas muscles are shortened when you are sitting. In fact, most of us spend most of our lives sitting. This results in our psoas shortening and being slightly contracted.

When you walk, you have what is called contralateral motion. This means that when your left leg swings when walking, your right arm also swings, counteracting the swing from your leg. Why does this need to happen? The leg swing generates momentum that travels through the spine. If that is not counteracted with an arm swing, that momentum, that energy, becomes stuck and turns into tension and holding along the spine. Your psoas muscles are what help to generate that leg swing and keep the energy traveling up through the spine, allowing for a more graceful, fluid walk.

Because of years of shortening and contraction and, thus, not properly functioning psoas muscles, we tend to rely on our quadriceps (muscles on the front of the thigh) and adductors (muscles on the inside of the leg) more for hip flexion in walking. Hip flexion is one of their actions but is not the primary one. Your psoas muscles' primary function is hip flexion. When you are mainly using your quadriceps and adductors in walking, each stride is a bit shortened and there is more pull and strain on your lower back, resulting in less fluid ease and gliding.

We live in a hustle-bustle world of constant distractions from cellphones, traffic, and continual noise. We are almost always in a low-level fight-or-flight response. The psoas muscles tense up when we respond that way. So, not only are they shortened from sitting, but they are also under a load of stress because of this anxious world we live in. The psoas muscle is related to fear and when it is contracted and tight, we tend to be more reactive and fearful.

By restoring balance to your psoas muscles, you are likely to release pent-up tension, which can have a profound effect on releasing unfounded fearfulness about life. You can release anxiety and be more aligned structurally, emotionally, and energetically all through stretching out your psoas muscles.

It was during that twilight walk, which I referenced just a bit ago, when I realized I had been pretending most of my life for fear of having my most vulnerable and most genuine self rejected. My ability to make this connection and have such a profound experience in my body came from the work I had received on my psoas muscles, allowing them to open and release years of holding. My very sense of being, how I showed up in the world and how I felt in the world, was directly linked to my psoas health. It has been called "the muscle of the soul," and I refer to it as that for this reason.

I Am Authentic

After supporting one of my clients to release some of her own posturing, she observed that she was moving much differently. She noticed that she was not only standing taller but felt more elegant and regal in her body, and walking was strangely effortless. She felt she was moving like a much younger version of herself, around ten years old, before physical injuries and torment from the external world got to her.

On an emotional level, she felt calmer, more joyous, and more open. She felt more connected to herself while at the same time, more a part of her community. When old memories surfaced, instead of feeling bothersome, they felt resolved and healed. For the first time in more than fifty years, she finally felt like herself in her body. Finally, she was at home and at peace in her skin.

Even if you have endured years of pain or hate toward your body, this feeling of effortlessness and ease is possible for you. Learning to connect to different energy centers in your body and how to properly stack your bones through simple anatomy will empower you to discover your body's inherent support. Yielding to this support will retrain your nervous system that you are safe and that you can stay present in your body. This will make it much easier to show up authentically.

Scary Vulnerability

If you want to show up in the world from an open-hearted place, you must first experience safety and security in your body. When you show up in your authentic posture and share your feelings honestly with others, they won't see you as weak or incompetent, as many of us fear, but instead will see you as courageous.

Years after that transformative walk, I was out on another walk (gentle nudge here for you to go walking, as it can be where magic happens for your body and soul). A woman called out from her porch, "You have beautiful posture!" I wasn't in my usual posturing or needing to prove anything through my structure. Instead, it was just me out on a walk enjoying the grace, fluidity, and uprightness of my body. And wow, it felt good to be acknowledged for that.

I hope this story serves as a reminder to allow yourself to simply *be*, to show up as you are in any given moment. Remember, true strength and acceptance come from within. And notice if you are posturing, acknowledge it, get curious about what it is you are protecting yourself from, and then if it feels safe and if you feel ready, let some of it go.

All of us must feel safe and at home in our bodies. The need is even more pressing if you have experienced significant trauma. You are likely to dissociate whether you've experienced a more significant trauma, like sexual or physical abuse, or even more minor trauma like someone pulling out in front of you when you are driving. This trauma, big T or little t, leaves us feeling unsafe, so we leave our bodies, creating a void within ourselves as our energy and attention go outside of us.

So, how can you teach your nervous system to understand you are safe? You can by spending more time in your body, little by little. With a retrained nervous system, you can show up more vulnerably and authentically. And, with time, the more you inhabit your body, the more acceptance, love, and reverence you will naturally experience toward it.

PRACTICE

Finding Safety and Security in Your Own Body

For a free guided audio of this practice, go to www.wishallwellness.com/radical-embodiment-free-gift.

This practice builds on How to Sit with Natural Alignment. If you have been practicing sitting on a regular basis, you may find it easier to feel some of the connections here. If you haven't been practicing, that's totally okay. Still give this practice a go. Know that I am beginning to layer more awareness exercises together, so go at your own pace. Experiencing one layer at a time can be useful.

Structurally, your heart is above your pelvis. If you can access the inherent support of your pelvis (which you have been doing through the pelvic cues in How to Sit with Natural Alignment as well through connecting into your womb space), you can learn to allow your heart to surrender into that support, enabling it to not be so protected.

When we share vulnerably, we are coming from our heart, but our heart wants to keep us safe, it wants to stay protected. When you can inhabit your pelvis more fully, you increase the ability of your pelvis to be of support. Your rib cage, which houses your heart, is going to be able to surrender and relax. You don't have to hold your heart and chest up; instead, your heart can rest into the center point of your pelvis. You won't have to hold it all together to protect yourself.

In this practice, we are connecting the center point of your heart and the center of your pelvis (your center of gravity). They get to move together in unison and be in communication with each other.

Utilizing the tips from How to Sit with Natural Alignment, sit down and make sure both of your feet are on the ground. Close your eyes. Feel your feet connecting into the earth beneath you. Let your breath come down into your lower abdomen.

Now, imagine the center point of your pelvis. Think of your pelvis as a bowl. Visualize a light in the center of it and bring your attention to that space. Imagine you are inhabiting your entire pelvic bowl with your focal point on the center point of your pelvis.

Next, bring your awareness to your heart. Take a few long moments to see if you can sense your heart, feeling into the space between your sternum and between your shoulder blades (mid-thoracic spine). This area tends to be held up in our posturing efforts. There is a lot of armoring that happens here that then limits our ability to show up authentically. Let this part of your body relax.

Staying connected and anchored into the center point of your pelvis, imagine your heart surrendering into that space. Bring your breath into your upper chest to help support you in finding this softening. Notice that your neck doesn't have to grip on so much, as it is held from below.

In this position, try the affirmation "I am authentic," or another statement that honors your genuineness. You can speak the words out loud and feel their vibrations in your body.

In my own experience relaxing into this space, it is what allows me to show up vulnerably but not leave a situation wondering "What did I say?," "Was I judged?," or like I gave too much of my energy. I feel able to share openly because I'm connected to the support underneath me. Emotionally and energetically, I feel safe. Increased vulnerability leads to more connection. Contact with others still might feel scary, but it can also feel really safe because you are not leaving yourself. You are here. You are home.

CHAPTER 8

Step Five
Tap into Desire

Limiting Belief: I Am Wrong

I have memories of being a little girl, watching *Land Before Time*, and underneath my blanket, I was quietly rubbing my crotch on the couch beneath me. I didn't know what I was doing, except that it felt good and I should be secretive about it. Once I was old enough to read, I snuck my family's "S" encyclopedia into my bedroom to secretly read about sex. In the sex section, it mentioned masturbation. Aha, so that's what I had been doing these past few years.

The encyclopedia went on to share how the Catholic Church viewed masturbation as a sin. This blew my Catholic kid mind. Hold up, what? What I had really been doing was sinning? This was no good. I had so much desire within me, and it felt fantastic.

My solution: I would get married at a super young age. I was eight. I did the math; ten years from then I would be eighteen, legal to get married. That's what I would do. Having sex outside of marriage is not only viewed as a sin but also a mortal (very bad) sin within the Catholic Church. I convinced myself that I could wait ten years until I was technically old enough to be married. Certainly, I could abstain from masturbation and sex and then get married young and enjoy sex within the confines of marriage and be a proper, good Catholic girl, right?

Wrong.

Suppressing my sexuality was a significant piece of what I believe led me to overeating. I have one vivid memory where I hid myself in my closet with my Christmas stocking full of chocolate. I gorged the chocolate in a hurried state, not wanting anyone to find me in my shameful, wrong state. One may call this gluttony; that is, over-indulgence or over-consumption. Gluttony is yet another mortal sin in the Catholic Church. Damn, one more way I was sinful.

I never told anyone my encyclopedia discovery moment or how I used to hide myself in my closet with food until recent years. I didn't want to be deemed "bad" or be disapproved of by my family. I wanted to remain the sweet good little Emily, the baby of the family.

I tried my best at being a prudent, good little Catholic girl. I really did. I told myself how sinful I was for those wants, how wrong I was. I tried to punish myself. My understanding was that pleasure was wrong. Sinful. In this life, to be "good" meant to suffer. I understood this disordered eating of chowing down on my Christmas chocolate, hidden away in my closet, to be sinful and bad and that I mustn't ever tell another soul about it. And so, the deep web of shame began to weave through me.

Good Girls Have Small Appetites

I felt wrong for having a big appetite. Wrong for shoving down all my Christmas candy. I felt wrong for feeling sexual. I felt wrong for being too fat.

As a young girl who wanted to be "good" so I could win the approval of others and feel as if I belonged, I thought I shouldn't want too much and felt wrong for my wanting. It makes sense then that the next natural thing for me to do was to suppress. If I pushed down my excessive desires, then I could be good. Sadly, no.

When you reject a part of yourself, that aspect of you does not go away. Instead, it comes out in a disordered way, like hiding in my closet eating my Christmas candy to push down and numb my desire.

Many of us subconsciously hold the belief that being "girly" or feminine is having a small appetite, eating delicately and only an appropriately limited amount. We are not to hunker down hungry for a full meal or be ravenous in our sexual appetite. Society wants us to squelch our appetites for food and for life and obsess over our bodies, trying with all our might to be thin so we may be loved and accepted.

Here are untrue, degrading, and limiting beliefs that hang around the subconscious of the feminine:

- An admirable woman who is worthy of respect should only eat a small amount of food. She should eat slowly and chew thoughtfully.
- A woman who is worthy of being held in high regard should have an appropriate appetite around sex. She shouldn't feel too much sexual desire or have constant thoughts about sex, as that is a thing for the guys, not for a lady.
- A proper woman shouldn't want too much in her life. She shouldn't crave more out of her career or her relationships,

> and she shouldn't seek more acknowledgment. She should be happy and grateful for what she has and work hard and be her most reverent self so that she can prove to herself and others that she is worthy of more.

So many of the women I work with have been conditioned since childhood to feel wrong for their body's natural reaction to release tears after being hurt or feeling upset. We are conditioned to not ask for too much or be too emotional. Don't cry, and if you do, you best go in your room and do so in private. Stay quiet, stay small.

I call bullshit.

Hunger Is Healthy

Everyone has a deep biological hunger to be part of the tribe. It is ingrained in us. We are hungry to belong. If we fear that voicing what we truly want will make us outcasts, we will instead do whatever it takes to feel as though we do belong. Often, doing "whatever it takes" involves something along the lines of not letting your needs be known and not allowing anyone to witness your full appetites for food or for life.

Your hunger isn't wrong. Sexual hunger, hunger for food, hunger for justice, hunger for a different life are your body's way of sharing something with you. It is a messenger.

Suppression, Shame, Controlling, and Restricting

Anytime you suppress anything, that behavior or feeling then becomes amplified. This is where compulsion and the feeling that you are out of control come from.

The soundtrack I was internally repeating to myself growing up was how wrong and fundamentally flawed I was for my feelings of intense desire. When you believe and continuously repeat (even on a subconscious level) a limiting belief, this creates pattern overlays in your mental and physical make-up.

Instead of allowing yourself to feel what you feel and to want what you want, you cover yourself with rigid structures to hide your imperfections and have only your appropriate parts be seen. This is all because you have concluded, from what you have seen and heard, that your truest self is wrong.

The key is to notice and allow your wants. Whatever they may be. Now, that doesn't mean you necessarily act on them although, if you do, know that you are not wrong and you should release any self-judgment that may arise. If you make a choice that you feel mixed about, make it and move on.

You must clear any judgment that what you want or desire is wrong. In place of that, allow yourself to feel your wish for pleasure. Feeling it and then talking about it clears the shame. Otherwise, it gets suppressed and hidden away in your fascia and tissues, and it will then come out as disordered eating, excessive exercise, feelings of general body hate, and pain.

Allowing yourself to experience and be seen in the full spectrum of your humanity is a gift to all but most importantly to yourself.

What You Resist Persists

I'm sure you have heard the above phrase before, but it is true and well worth repeating.

Why are you resisting eating? Why are you resisting feeling? Why are you resisting expressing? Restrictions build rigidity. They create more narrowing of our minds and linear ways of thinking. Your mind becomes obsessed with the restriction. It builds superiority around the restriction.

For example, if you restrict yourself from eating cookies and have labeled them as bad or wrong, and then you do happen to have a craving for a cookie, immediate judgment of how bad you are will occur. If you eat that forbidden food, god help you. And according to your linear path, there are two ways you could be moving: up (progress) or down (regression). So, I guess that bite of cookie means you are regressing and there is no hope for you, so you may as well binge. Tomorrow, you will do better. Tomorrow, you will restrict more. More control, that's what you need. You've been too easy on yourself.

These seem like appropriate behaviors toward our unruly wants, right? Wrong.

The more you try to control a behavior and the more you try to control yourself as though you are an unruly, wild beast who needs to be caged, the more that beast will want to break free and run amok.

When you resist, you may be able to quiet the craving, urge, or desire for a short bit, but I can guarantee it will come knocking again and usually more loudly. Instead of resisting, get curious. Cravings want to tell you something. What is this craving about? What is this urge for gorging out on dessert really trying to tell me? What is my longing for sex really wanting me to know?

Journal this. Write it out. You can create a sort of dialogue. This may seem silly, but really, write out a dialogue, kind of like a play script with your voice and the voice of the craving. Ask the craving if it has a name. Ask it what it wants you to know. Do your best to remain in a state of curiosity here. Keep asking questions. You may be quite surprised what answers come out from your hand. This will help you receive clarity and insight on the root of the desire.

Permission and Desire

We are humans. In human bodies. Living a human experience. Human stuff happens. Life's tough. Soften the grip and give yourself some room. Grant permission for gluttony and for self-soothing.

Give yourself permission to feel what you feel, want what you want, and to eat what you desire. Allow yourself to be okay with your body as is. Tell yourself it's okay to let go of the incessant chore of fixing your body's appearance. Grant yourself the right to experience more pleasure. When you give yourself permission, there is a relaxation that happens. It allows for more ease.

For us women, if we give ourselves permission to feel our desire, we become more powerful. We become clearer on our vision. There's a natural swing from doing less to being more. We don't get so lost in all the to-dos, feeling scattered and overwhelmed. We are clear in our direction. We don't feel so stuck in patterns of projection and perfection.

You will experience greater ease in your thoughts and in your body the more you own your desires and sit in how good it feels when you connect into them. Because you aren't suppressing your wants, you will have more space. Instead of being tight and restricted like the rubber band analogy I shared earlier, you will have more room inside (emotionally and physically), more space to make a different choice, one toward loving and honoring your body.

You may have a strategy to keep from feeling desire. Maybe you busy yourself or numb yourself through a substance. When you truly connect with your desires, the sensation can be uncomfortable because it will actively shed light on the aspects of your life that aren't working well. Your desires will ask of you to have courage, strength, and perseverance to shake some shit up in your life.

Maybe you say, "As long as I say I don't know what I want, I don't have to risk." When you don't connect with how you feel, you will be unclear on what you want, and thus, you will be able to stay safe and comfortable.

The feelings of overwhelm that are all too easy for all of us to experience these days as we stay glued to our phones and the Internet are also keeping us safe. If you feel overloaded, there is no space to think about your true desires. You need to take a nap or self-soothe. You don't have the energy to look at what is ready to be uncovered. That would require stillness and risk.

So, as I have shared before, most of us have created a pattern of being out of our body, the body we loathe. We spend more time in our heads stuck in thought, worry, and projected fear.

Instead of punishing your body for being wrong by creating more restrictions, what if you indulged in it? Like, how would it be if you went into full-on luxuriating mode? What if you became a glutton for your body? Not superficially, with exterior indulgences like food, sex, or alcohol but with internal sensual satiation.

Your options to celebrate your body are limitless. The important thing is your intent. The gesture of treating yourself this way has more to do with your attitude than the activity itself. Taking a bath can be a sacred gift to the self or it can be another "should" adopted from some self-care list.

When was the last time you showed your body some love? I mean like real love. When was the last time you rubbed oil over your entire body, savoring the contact with your own skin? (More on this at the practice at the end of this chapter.) When did you last take deep pleasure in each skin cell being hydrated, touched, acknowledged, and saturated? Celebrate your body's extraordinariness!

The challenge is giving yourself what is all too often seen in our societal, cultural, and religious beliefs as "indulgent," "selfish," and "sinful." The challenge is shifting from operating like your body is bad and needs to be controlled to viewing your body as a holy altar.

The truth is ecstasy is your birthright. Denying yourself *true* pleasure is the real sin as *that* is where manipulative, controlling, conniving, and compulsive behaviors come from.

What Are Your Go-to Pleasure Givers?

Create a list of things that give you pleasure. Keep the list near you. Each day, gift yourself at least one thing from your list. This way you are continuously feeling some bit of pleasure and not letting your tank get depleted. Again, this suggestion is not meant to become another "should" but rather something you are excited to do. When you have moments of feeling triggered, rely on your list. Pick whatever feels simplest and most desirable at that time. Gift your body the satiation of pleasure from things that enhance your well-being.

My current list of pleasure givers:

- Float tanks
- My Spotify playlists
- Putting my phone on airplane mode
- Soft density foam rolling
- Lying on tennis balls
- Acupuncture
- Saunas
- Hot springs/hot tubs/hot water
- Hula hooping
- Being around kids
- Spending time in nature
- Guided meditation when I am positioned up on pillows and a blanket
- Cute videos of animals and, if I really want to open my heart, stories of animals being rescued
- Dancing

Track what makes your body moan, what makes it exhale in pleasure. Do more of that.

Let Yourself Receive (and Indulge)

Often, particularly for women, when we celebrate ourselves, we are seen as egotistical or arrogant.

When you let yourself fully receive, feeling what you're taking in on a cellular level, you experience more satiation and contentment. When you move on from one experience to the next, crossing off one to-do then on to the next one, without really acknowledging yourself for the work you put in, you deprive yourself of an incredibly rich gift. Celebrating your steps in the right direction is what can motivate you forward. *You deserve to bask in your incredibleness.* Savor it.

Let yourself receive compliments and well wishes from others and absorb your own celebrations throughout the day, recognizing how awesome you are and how much you love your body for being able to do what it can do. Honor yourself for conquering that intense workout, going up and down the stairs, finishing your swim when your mind wanted to override the experience because you didn't have that much time. Receiving fills you up. Don't miss out on savoring this goodness. Don't block yourself from allowing this in because this is what calls in more satisfaction and contentment.

PRACTICE
The Pleasure of Self-massage

This practice introduces you to *abhyanga*, self-massage. It is used in the Indian Ayurvedic tradition to promote physical wellness. This form of massage is also a wonderful way to tell your body you cherish it and to really let yourself receive the gift of your own touch.

Bring your awareness into your body and run through your powerful centers: your womb space and heart space. As it is done in the Ayurvedic tradition, warm a small amount of oil, and rub it into your skin, head to toe. Go slowly. As you massage yourself, say your affirmations, feeling their juicy vibration. Spend longer on the areas of your body you have historically hated. Send those parts of you love and gratitude. This is you reclaiming those parts of you, reintegrating them into your system. Let this self-massage be pleasurable and feel really good. As you massage, say the affirmations you have been working with thus far. You can also add in these new ones: "Pleasure is my birthright" or "I am built for delight."

When you are finished, taking your sweet precious time, sit for at least five minutes in silence, rooted in your womb space. Feel your radiance.

Add this to your weekly routine. Do it in a warm room with candles and dim lighting. This is particularly nice to do after a warm shower or bath.

CHAPTER 9

Step Six

Let Yourself Be Fully Seen

Limiting Belief: I Am Too Much

Most of my life my pattern was to jump out of my body and take up as little space as possible. I tried to cover up my thighs from a young age. I remember being at a Brownie's meeting. My Brownie leader was crouched on the floor in a low squat. The memory is vivid for me of noticing her legs and how she didn't have much fat at all on her thighs, particularly in the area right by the knee. I looked down at my own legs in a similar position. I felt ashamed of the amount of flesh present at that same spot and, what I deemed to be, the large size of my own thighs. I remember feeling sad thinking it was too bad I couldn't sit in that low squat position because it made my thighs look too big.

At some point in later high school, I stopped wearing shorts and rarely wore jeans or pants. I discovered I could conceal my thighs better under skirts and dresses. I believed my legs were too big for the world, that if I let them be seen, people wouldn't approve of me and I would be rejected. I imagined away my body, I took shallow breaths, I did everything possible to keep my flaws hidden, to keep them held in.

If you have the sense that you are too much, whether physically, emotionally, energetically, or spiritually, you will naturally and subconsciously start to limit your breath. You will breathe more shallowly, reducing your oxygen intake as you strive to occupy less space.

Now, my legs are strong. The build of my body is curvy with wide hips and large thighs. The constant desire to hide that part of my body is no longer there. I feel quite proud of my thighs. They help me climb up mountains and ski. They enable me to walk, stand, and support myself through each day. My mind no longer torments me with why oh why are my thighs so big. Instead, I enjoy getting to celebrate them!

This important shift is an internal one: finding, owning, and claiming my validation from the inside, from my Self! Little by little through the years I have released the need for external validation. I get to *own* and *claim* my space and power and do so while being supported from my tremendously strong, beautiful thighs. I get to allow my body to take up the space it occupies. I get to embody my messy whole self instead of dissociating. I get to inhabit myself fully.

I Am Too Much

How many times have these words or a close variation run through your head?

My needs are too much. My hair/stomach/thighs/arms/butt are too much. My body is too much. My desires are too much. I am too much.

Every single female client of mine has some sort of struggle around being "too much." One may consider her needs to be too much in her relationship. Another feels as if the salary she wants to ask for at work is too much. On top of that, unfortunately, every single woman I know, professionally or personally, believes some aspect of her body is too much.

A Rolfing experience with a client comes to mind. In the session, we released a lot of holding in my client's hips. When she got off the table, she was smiling about her newfound sense of freedom and movement in her hips. But, as she started to walk around, a look of concern came over her. She shared that she wasn't sure if all this new hip movement was okay. She wondered if it was too sexual and too much. She didn't want to attract unwanted attention or have people thinking, "Who does she think she is?'

My client said that when she was in middle school, someone had given her feedback that she shouldn't let her hips move so freely because it would send the wrong impression to young men. So, she purposefully controlled her hips and restricted her legs from swinging easily. This created years of lower back and hip pain for her.

I invited her to keep walking back and forth in my office, allowing the full movement of her hips. I wanted her to notice how this motion felt in her body, what was different, and what she had been holding in her body before to prevent it.

Because this new way of walking felt overtly sexual to her, I suggested she play walking with her hips moving freely in front of the mirror over the next week. That way, she could see herself moving in this way and determine for herself in the safety of her own home if it was too sexy or not. In my well-trained eye, it was not sexual in the least. Instead, her body was walking as it should and her low back was happy to be free for the first time in years.

Your Needs Are Not Too Much

Where does this belief of "I am too much" stem from? A part of it comes from how those around you responded to your emotions when you were a little girl. When you cried, what happened? Were you told to stop feeling sorry for yourself and go to your room? Were you called a "crybaby"?

A coaching client of mine had the belief that her needs were too much when in a relationship. She believed what she really wanted was too needy and no man could meet her needs. As we worked together, we uncovered this belief coming from her childhood. When she was a girl and would cry, her mom told her to stop being so emotional and dramatic. She would get sent to her room for her tears. When she would ask for something, anything from a new toy to her mom's attention, she was met with anger and frustration. The story my client internalized was that she couldn't ask for what she really wanted and needed, her needs really were too much, and she was just too emotional. She noticed the trend in her relationships was that she never fully expressed her needs and, instead, shrank down and became small.

Because she had the old wound of feeling as if her needs were too much, she also went above and beyond to take care of what she perceived as the needs of others. She is a single mom, and gave, gave, gave to her children. She loved them but never felt they appreciated her. She yearned to be in a committed partnership; therefore, in her dating relationships, she gave, gave, and gave. Again, she never had the sense she was fully valued or reciprocated. On an energetic level, she would unconsciously leave herself and go into others' fields to help them feel better, to comfort them, to give them some of her energy. The result had her moving through life feeling exhausted, neglected, and like there was no room for her.

Working together, I was able to support her first in seeing this pattern. You must first notice and become aware of a pattern so you can create a pattern interrupt to stop that trend. Because her needs and wants were constantly rejected and ignored as a young child, my client had adopted the smart strategy of never knowing how she felt. If she didn't know how she felt, she wouldn't really need anything or could more easily go with the flow of what her mom wanted. In her adult life, this showed up as her being aware of how everyone else felt and what she perceived they needed. She'd care for them, but this comfortable pattern she created to help her feel safe left her feeling unappreciated and not seen. I worked with this client to connect with her body and allow herself to land into the resonance of her internal sensations.

From there, we worked with her, noticing how she felt, emotionally, physically, and energetically. She continued this practice multiple times a day. After she uncovered how she felt, she would ask herself, "Based on how I'm feeling, what would help me feel just a little bit better?" Doing this enabled her to acknowledge how she was truly feeling, never bypassing or pushing down any desires or emotions. It also supported her in clarifying what she wanted and strengthened her awareness to notice more quickly, in relationships or around her children, when she had popped out of her energetic field and into theirs. She was able to recognize what she was truly feeling in her current relationship and communicate that feeling to her man in a way he could receive.

Anytime you suppress your needs or wants because they feel too much, you are pushing away a part of yourself. Rejecting a significant piece of who you are is painful. To cover up this pain, to distract yourself from what you are really feeling, is where patterns of disordered eating, popping out of yourself, etc., begin to be created.

We feel we are not enough while simultaneously feeling we are too much. The irony.

Validation for Being Small

We receive so much validation from others and the world the second we lose weight. The minute you change your physical body in some way that makes it appear more acceptable to the external eye, which usually involves becoming smaller, you receive praise. Seriously, every time I have lost weight, someone says, "Wow, you look like you've lost some weight. You look great." Which in turn always makes my mind wonder: Did I not look great before? Did those five or ten pounds really make me look that horrible? Of course, these are well-meaning folks, but if you have struggled with your body image most of your life, comments on your weight don't feel good.

Recently a client I hadn't seen in months came in. I noticed she looked slimmer, but more than that I saw a certain new elasticity in her tissue. Her fascia felt more available, hydrated, and ready to release. This is what I chose to comment on, that I noticed something different in her tissue. Right or wrong, I don't know, but I know I am so over having my weight commented on that I do my best to not comment on others. We are so much more than a number on the scale. Losing weight can be tremendously supportive for your overall well-being, but when we're made to feel as if it's our most important accomplishment, this is really a disservice to all.

Feeling Yourself

This one may sound a bit kinky, but, I promise, it's completely G-rated.

When a woman begins to take up more space, she is often met with some criticism. People in her life saying she is "full of herself" and "Who does she think she is?"

In Chapter Six, I talked about how you have a physical and an energetic body. All things have energy. Think of when someone sends you good "vibes" or is thinking of you. I'm sure you know people who inexplicably make you feel nervous. There are also those people who relax you. This is your own energy field reacting and responding to theirs.

Think about where your own energy is. Is it in your field and in your body, or is it out lost in thought loops? If your energy is not contained within you and the sphere around you, you are leaving voids for others' energies to come in and fill. If you don't take up your space, someone else will.

Have you ever felt icky after leaving a conversation or walking out of a store? Often, that "ickiness" is someone else's energy that has come into your sphere. Do you know the kinds of people who, when they are talking to you, cause you to want to step back? They are right up in your space, so excited about what they want to share with you that they are completely uncontained with their own energy. The more voids you have in your own field (the less you are inhabiting your body), the more room you are leaving for others to come in and claim your space.

A few years back, I was working with a client who was a professor at a local university. She shared that she felt overlooked and not respected amongst her colleagues, most of whom happened to be male. We spent one session specifically working with her connecting first into her womb space and, from there, expanding out through what I would call her energy field. The following weekend, she was speaking at a conference. Normally when she spoke, afterward she would feel like no one really acknowledged her and would receive feedback that she needed to speak louder.

As she spoke, she could feel herself taking up more space than she ever had before. She felt confident and at ease. After her talk, several of her male colleagues, whom she felt normally barely noticed her, came up to share how much they enjoyed her presentation and wanted to continue the dialogue. This woman is maybe five-foot-two and petite, but in her own words, when she gave this talk, she felt like the largest person in the room.

When you are connecting to your energy field, having the intention to do this automatically lights it up. You are giving yourself permission to take up space and be seen. You aren't shrinking away or diffusing your potency. Instead, you are circulating your incredibly powerful energy back to and through you. You don't need to give your energy to anyone else.

As you become practiced at this, you will find that you naturally experience more acceptance and love for yourself. You won't feel so sapped at the end of a workday or time with family (or insert draining event of your choice) because you will have an energetic boundary that is malleable that moves with you as you navigate in and out of different spaces and around other people. You will feel more full of love and energy.

When you inhabit your own space (your physical body and energy field), you are claiming your power and allowing in all aspects of your humanity. Any old habitual perceptions that you are insignificant, don't belong, or shouldn't be taking up space will more readily pass.

As I worked on this practice for myself, I was startled to find a new expansiveness in my body and in my energy. I had access to a level of joy I hadn't before. There is so much pleasure to be found within your own body and energetic field. Literally feeling yourself feels so damn good!

As you read this, take a moment and shake your hands in the air. Now stop. Can you feel the tingly vibration within them? This is your internal energetic field. Where else in your body are you able to feel this?

When you take up your own space, you not only feel good, but you also become much clearer on what energy is yours versus others' and you have the insight to know what it is you really want. In the case of the client I discussed above, the professional single mom who believed her needs were too much, there was no clear border around her energetic field, so she diffused her energy. This left her prey for others' energy to come in, which in turn led to her being confused about what she truly felt or wanted.

When you connect with your energy field, expanding it but keeping it contained just for you, you will develop greater acceptance and love for your body and experience more confidence, ease, and peace.

PRACTICE

Taking Up Your Space[3]

This practice is designed to help you own and claim your energetic space instead of shrinking, diffusing out, or giving too much and not having boundaries. Because many of us have been made to feel wrong for "being too much," we don't inhabit all of our space. The more you are aware and present of your energy field, the more you will be seen, the clearer your boundaries are, and, honestly, the better you will feel.

Stand with feet shoulder width apart. Bring your arms out to your sides. Your energy field is about an arm's length out (about two to three feet) from you in all directions: to the sides, behind you, on top of you, and below you.

First, start by connecting and grounding into your womb space. See if you can feel the energy from your womb space moving down your legs and moving up through your torso out through your arms.

Can you feel a tingling sensation within your body? In your arms? Down your legs?

Once you feel connected to your internal energetic presence, I invite you to expand it out, growing big. It may help to anchor into your womb space again and invite your energy field to grow larger, moving out from your pelvis in the front and the back. Imagine your

3 The above practice is a modified practice based on the work of Rachael Jayne Groover, the creator of the Art of Feminine Presence, Light Globe practice.

energy field expanded out in all directions an arm's length around you. Become aware of its edge, of its border, where it stops.

It can be helpful (but perhaps feel silly to do) to move your arms in all directions to help you have a tangible sense how large your energy field is.

Now, feel your energy flowing through you, out of you, and bouncing back to you once it meets the border of your energy field. How does it feel to be large, expanded, and contained?

Simply by making the conscious decision to become more aware of your energy field, you are lighting yourself up. Owning and having an awareness of this space will support you in taking up more space and being seen.

CHAPTER 10

Step Seven

Experience Your Inherent Worthiness

Limiting Belief: I Am Not Worthy

This is how I felt my first winter living in Boulder. I knew only a handful of people. I weighed about twenty pounds more than I do now. This fact isn't bad, but the reason behind the additional weight is the reason I am mentioning it. I was caught in the vicious thought cycle of believing I wasn't worthy.

I was depressed. I was insecure and ashamed in my body.

I felt tired, alone, and overwhelmed. Going to any event gave me a great burst of anxiety. If I made it inside, my mind was often loud with negative self-talk. I would think, "Why'd I say that?" or "I sound stupid," or I'd hide in a corner somewhere (when I came to the event with the intention to "network'). Often, I wouldn't even make it inside to the gathering. My mind would come up with some highly believable reason for why I shouldn't go, convincing me out of it so I would not have to face my anxiety and insecurities.

I was *stuck*.

Intellectually, I knew what I *should* be eating. I knew that I *should* be having more positive thoughts, be saying my affirmations. I knew that I *should* be getting regular exercise. But I didn't know how to get there. I felt powerless, disconnected, afraid, and ashamed. I'd tell friends and family I was "happy" when really, I felt dull and alone on the inside.

Deep down, I didn't believe I was worthy of incredible friendships or enjoyment of my days. I didn't feel worthy to charge what I was worth professionally. I didn't feel worthy of dating the men I was truly attracted to.

I struggled with compulsive overeating. I would get off from my job as a nanny, make a pit stop to the grocery store, and buy a couple containers of cookies and candy bars. I had about a fifteen-minute drive home and the compulsion to shove food in my mouth was so strong, I always got something that I could eat while I was driving. I would get to my house, hide away in my room, and curl up next to some show with my food.

There were days when I felt all right, and then seemingly out of nowhere, the compulsion to overeat would hit. I felt outside of my body and completely out of control. One day, I had a ridiculously strong craving for Oreos. I kept trying to ignore and push the craving away until finally it was so strong, I found myself in my car headed toward the grocery store. Somehow, I caught myself. I pulled over and started tapping, attempting to bring myself back to some sort of peace and sanity. If you're unfamiliar with tapping, the website for The Tapping Solution Foundation describes the practice as ". . . tapping with your fingertips on specific meridian points while talking through traumatic memories and a wide range of emotions."

It is designed to restore the body's energy balance and move beyond lower vibration emotions.

I remember this moment vividly. I was parked in my red Honda Accord on some random side street. I tapped to soothe my intense craving for Oreos. This helped settle me for a bit. The compulsion for the immediate fix for the Oreos lessened a little. I felt proud of myself. And yes, this was something to celebrate: I had made it home sans Oreos!

But then throughout the evening, all I could think about was those Oreos. I don't quite recall the rest, but at some point, I went and got the fucking Oreos. I felt so ashamed of myself. I felt so wrong. I hated feeling this out of control. I loathed this compulsion. I felt so incredibly unworthy of anything I truly wanted.

Is the belief of "I am not worthy" holding you back? Is it keeping you from owning and sharing your expertise on a larger scale? Is it making you feel stuck in a loop of unhappiness and dissatisfaction? Do you feel undeserving of the relationships, be they romantic, friendships, and career, that you truly desire?

If you don't feel worthy, you get to stay comfortable. You don't have to risk much. You get to stay in your little bubble. But what you are missing out on from not *feeling* your worth is tremendous.

At this point in my life, I was in no way living my truth. I was out of alignment with my beliefs on what a healthful lifestyle looked like or felt like. I didn't believe I could make long-lasting changes. I didn't believe I had the strength or the courage.

I felt like a victim of my body and was disconnected from my integrity.

Integrity

When we get out of alignment with ourselves and our true life's purpose, an imbalance is generated. This imbalance then manifests on a physical, mental, and/or emotional level as pain, anxiety, unhappiness, fatigue, disease, and so on. Anytime we internalize shame about an action or something we said, we get pushed even further out of alignment. This is exactly what was happening to me.

I felt I had to over-exert myself to get things done. Every aspect of life felt too risky and hard, which is why I ran away from my desires and retreated to the comforts of my room and food.

Fast-forward a couple of years. I had made tremendous personal progress and growth but still felt significantly unworthy. In my first year of working for myself, I really struggled. Of course, the first year of any business is going to be challenging, but I internalized the struggle. Outwardly, I was projecting that I absolutely knew what I was doing. I would leave a gathering exhausted. I felt scattered, and often, like I couldn't find the ground beneath me. I was rigid, in my body and my mind. At this rate, I was going to burn out quickly.

Learning to inhabit my body, through the very practices that I share in this book, is what allowed me to *own* my essence. These practices enabled me to begin living in a way that *feels good* and is in integrity to me. Through this work, I began to feel safe in my body and was able to shift out of my hiding. They helped me release compulsive overeating, experience contentment, invite in community, and have truly meaningful and fulfilling relationships. I saw growth in my business but with less pushing and "hard work." Coming back into my body, time and time again, is what continues to bring me back into alignment.

What Does It Mean to Inhabit Your Body?

A huge difference exists between thinking about being in your body and being in your body. Embodiment is not an intellectual process. When I close my eyes and shift my attention down and in with the intention of entering every one of my cells, I feel a glorious sensation within my body. It is the same as the tingly vibrating of your energy field.

Making the conscious choice to be fully present in your body, experiencing and allowing in all sensations, increases your interoceptive awareness. Interoception is your perception of the internal state of your body. It is the mind-body connection that encompasses your ability to sense and regulate signals from inside your body, and it includes breathing, heartbeat, cravings, fatigue, and pain. Numerous studies have shown that mindful attention toward physical sensations from inside the body changes brain rhythms. There's a vast, intricate maze of neural circuits communicating these signals between your organs and your brain. Through approaches like the practices included in this book, you can strengthen your interoceptive awareness, which in turn improves your physical and emotional well-being.

You can actually measure your interoceptive awareness, so this embodiment talk isn't all just esoteric fluff. University of California San Francisco doctor Wolf Mehling, along with a team from the National Center for Complementary and Integrative Health, created the Multidimensional Assessment of Interoceptive Awareness (MAIA) scale to assess this aspect of self-perception. The researchers found that chronic pain patients who employed emotional awareness, self-regulation, body-listening, meditation, yoga, and tai chi were more likely to experience relief from their symptoms.

It is a gift to all when you reclaim your body. I hope with the practices at the end of each chapter and from my online meditations, you have had a chance to experience what it feels like to inhabit your body. It is time to rewrite the story of hating or even disliking your physical form. It is time to stop punishing yourself. That sort of behavior and mode of thought make any sort of change toward progress (progress in this case meaning you feel better and better and are coming more into your own true alignment) more difficult. Be gentle with your body. Welcome in what it is wanting to tell you.

Yes, this will be uncomfortable. Many of us have pain that has been hidden away in our tissue, pain we have never fully felt. Your body is incredibly wise and knows you weren't prepared to experience that pain at the time of the event, and so it muffled it. Now you have the resources and adaptability to *feel* that pain. You have the room in your body through these practices to allow the pain to move through you so that you can release it. This will create sooooo much freedom. You will feel lighter, more alert, and more capable, and you will have more patience. (If you have had significant trauma in your past that you haven't worked with and don't believe you have the capacity to tolerate what might emerge as you unlock it, please seek support from a therapist, coach, or other professional.)

You'll recall that when you have experienced trauma or when you are unhappy in your body, the automatic response is to dissociate. The more you can reclaim your body, little by little, the more you will become the driver of your life. Working incrementally with kindness toward yourself is crucial. If the womb space practice is too challenging for you right now, for instance, start with just being in your hands. Then, slowly begin to bring your attention to the lower half of your body. Can you be in your legs? This approach invites healing to happen at a pace that respects your past experiences.

Yours is the one body you get in this life. It is time to stop the distrust and dislike of it and start being gentle and compassionate with it. It is time to become curious about it, how it moves and how it feels. It is time to notice what parts of your body feel challenging to inhabit and what parts feel alive with sensation. I urge you to take deep pleasure in this miracle of flesh and bone, muscles and fascia.

Aligning Your Physical and Energetic Bodies

This is where you get to integrate *all* parts of yourself. You have a physical body and an energetic body. Some people tend to move in a physical way, and others move more energetically. When you move both together with focus and intention, your joy level increases. A balance between the two is where magic happens.

The work you are doing to connect with your energetic body, as well as the increased awareness you are gaining about how your physical body is feeling, will help to bring more integration between them both. The two aspects of you are intertwined. Your energetic body is continuously flowing through your physical body. I'd love for you to access a visceral experience of how this ecstatic physical-energetic space feels.

Why does integrating your physical and energetic bodies matter?

Because it allows you to reclaim your power. You get to reclaim the driver's seat of your body instead of being driven by your limiting beliefs. Bringing together these two parts of yourself is huge in healing the wounds around your body. It will support you in experiencing more acceptance for your body. Little by little, as you continue to practice, you will begin to feel true love for your body and for yourself.

You then get to move with love. You get to eat with love. You get to take care of yourself from a place of love. There is much more joy for you to experience. There is much more good to be done in the world, and your energy will be greater utilized to do it.

I've said it before, ecstasy is your birthright. You are meant to experience pleasure on a consistent basis. You don't have to keep searching outside of yourself for the great sensual and intangible joy you are capable of feeling. It is within you.

PRACTICE

Grant Yourself the Time and Space to Feel What You Feel

When we don't feel worthy, we don't grant ourselves the time, even if for a few moments, to ask ourselves how we really feel. I want you to begin a practice of asking yourself how you feel. This is a great practice to do throughout your day to check in on yourself, but at least one time a day, I would like you to commit to being able to spend a bit longer on this practice.

First, take your full deep belly breaths. Anchor into your womb space. Let your heart soften and relax from there. Next, connect into your energy field. Are you able to feel your internal energetic presence? Can you feel your energetic presence as it expands out from you?

Now, staying centered and grounded in your womb space, I want you to ask yourself the following questions, without judgment or needing to fix anything. You are simply becoming aware of how it is you are feeling.

For this practice, instead of an affirmation, I invite you to ask yourself these questions:

- How am I feeling emotionally?
- How am I feeling physically?
- How am I feeling energetically?

Let the answer arise from within.

Once you have connected with how you feel, ask yourself this: "Based on how I'm feeling, what would help me feel just a little bit better?" You can get a bit more specific with this question by adding: "for today," "in this moment," "in this conversation," "in this meeting," etc.

The intention here is not to jump up on the emotional scale but to slow the resistance train and see if you could move up a little bit. I find that when I ask myself what would help me feel a bit better, usually my answer is simple: I just want to stay connected to myself, staying grounded in my womb space. Sometimes, the answer is that I want something, perhaps to go for a walk, do some stretches, have a conversation with someone, but for me, in that moment, in that day, in that meeting, I usually want to stay connected to myself and in my body as much as possible, because for me, that always feels good.

Acknowledging and being with how you feel is one of the most beautiful ways of expressing your worthiness to yourself. You are owning your worth by giving yourself what you most want in that moment and are not pushing away any feelings.

CHAPTER 11

Bumps Along the Way

I am not against self-soothing. I am not against self-medicating. I am not against junk food. I am not against drinking. I am not against numbing. I am not against any of it.

I am also not necessarily for any of this. A purpose of this book is to empower readers with support and tools and shine the light of awareness on some of our ways of thinking, behaviors, and cultural norms that do not serve us.

I am for *awareness.* I am for *noticing.* I am for *curiosity.* I am for having *choices.*

If you do eat an extra slice of cake, a pint of ice cream, whatever it may be, and eat it in an effort to self-soothe and comfort yourself, don't be hard on yourself. That is clearly the opposite of what your system is needing. If you are seeking food (insert your chosen coping mechanism) for comfort, then once you have chosen it, be gentle with yourself. Hold yourself in compassion as that is incredibly soothing and may just be exactly what you need.

When Sweets Are Everywhere

What happens when there are donuts in the office? When it feels like cookies and candy are everywhere, do these feel like temptations to you? Let's reframe that.

Sweetness is good. We all want more sweetness. But sweetness does not have to come from sweets. It could come from a hug from a child, from enjoying the details of a tree on an afternoon walk, or from that cookie. And if it does come from a cookie, allow it. Don't feel guilty about it. Don't decide you are "so bad" or say things like, "I'm going to have to be good the rest of the week and work out extra because I've overindulged."

Stop punishing yourself for the choices you are making. Make the decision and move forward from it. If you eat a food you have typically labeled as bad, let yourself taste and savor it instead of shoving its badness into your mouth.

When the donuts in the office kitchen seem to be taunting you on a day when you feel tired and overwhelmed, let that be okay. Have a donut if it might help you feel better, but don't feel like you have no control over the donut. Notice how you feel. Ask yourself what would help you feel a little bit better in this moment. Is it the donut? Or is it taking a five-minute reprieve away from work and the screen and giving yourself some deep, full belly breaths?

Working with ourselves around sweets happens year-round. But when the holiday season arrives, it can be easy for old tricks of the mind to come in. You might think you should diet before the season gets started so you don't get too big. Or maybe you tell yourself that as soon as those parties end, you must diet to lose the three to five pounds you have gained. Instead of obsessing over your weight, shift your focus to how you feel. Are you energized and content? Are you tired? What shifts in your life could you make to help you feel a little bit better? Maybe that's eating a little cleaner and choosing foods you experience as nourishing. Maybe that's moving a bit more to get your heart rate up, release stress, and bring back some energy.

The external choices you make might look similar to ones you have made in the past when you believed you needed to diet and get your body under control, but the internal place of motivation that they are coming from is completely different.

Gentleness Is the Key

Along this journey of body love and along this journey of life, be easy on yourself. It is not your job, duty, or a "sign of success" for you to be hard on yourself. Lighten up. Relax and slow down more. Put your screen away. Spend time around children, animals, and the sun.

There is no perfect way. It is a process. Be patient with this work. Most importantly, be patient with yourself. Notice what you say to yourself. Would you tell that to a child? Would you say that to your lover or best friend? Be kinder to yourself. Be gentler.

As I was writing this book, my own outdated behaviors began to not only emerge but drive the show. There were times when the process felt like too much. My old habits that not only no longer felt good, but patterns I thought I had healed from, crept in as I dug up some of my most painful moments. I was reflecting a lot about all the disdain I have felt toward my body. I had waves of insecurity and uncertainty about putting myself out there as an expert on body love. I got snappy with my family. I was out of my comfort zone. I lost my own internal space for a bit.

I avoided writing by overeating, drinking too much wine, engaging in excessive mindless screen time, and completing every other task that was on my list that really wasn't urgent or pressing.

This is the truth. We are all human, and we have to start talking more about our shadow sides, about what have historically been our shameful behaviors. I'll share in more detail about working with your shadow in the next chapter.

I wanted to feel vital, present, and healthful as I wrote. But I also strongly desired to give myself permission to ride whatever wave came up. I finally said okay and allowed the avoidance, going with those comforting waves instead of resisting or pushing through them. Basically, I followed my own advice. I gave myself permission to feel my emotions without needing to create a story or requiring that feeling to change. When I felt sad, I let myself move slowly in my sadness for a few days.

As much as this writing activated so many insecurities within me and at times felt like a struggle, it was also an incredible gift to be fortunate enough to write. There were multiple days when cocooning myself up to write felt oh so comforting. It was cathartic and healing.

After I allowed myself to avoid and became gentle with myself in how that manifested, I began to shift naturally into taking exquisite care of myself. I'd foam roll and stretch before sitting down to write. I took time off from social media and away from my phone. Every day I moved in some way, elevating my heart rate and making sure I worked up a sweat when I felt low. I walked and took hikes with my pup, Tula Rose, leaving my phone at home. I sat in the sun, enjoying its warmth on my skin.

I created space for lots of internal healing. I took loads of baths, meditated, and journaled. I received as much as I could: Rolfing, craniosacral work, massages, the listening ears of friends, and solace and comfort in the float tank. I did the things I know felt good to me and promoted my well-being.

Reconciling with Resistance

When you begin being gentle with yourself, you may wonder if you are giving in to complacency. You may question if it truly is okay to love yourself as you are before you meet the weight loss and physique goals. You may sense pressure from society to push harder and hustle more. This resistance is arising to support you. It challenges you to experience stronger resolve in your decision to shift from body hating to acceptance and then to operating from love. These questions are coming up to have you look a bit deeper and uncover the roots of some of your habitual ways of thinking.

When life feels hard or you feel overwhelmed, stressed, sad, or lonely, what will you choose to make yourself feel a little bit better? How will you self-soothe?

If you choose your old limiting coping strategies, please don't be too tough on yourself. Be kind and compassionate. The negative punishment and talk not only feels bad, but it also doesn't work. Continue to positively reinforce yourself.

If you diverge down a limiting slope, *notice*. See if you can do something to interrupt the behavior or thought. Go to another room in the house. Dance to your favorite song. Do ten burpees or jumping jacks. Give yourself a hug or gently pat your shoulders. Action is the way of progression. Even if you are having a bumpy night, day, week, month, or year, what movements in the right direction can you see? Own those. Don't talk yourself down.

Moving in the Right Direction (MITRD)

The growth and healing process is not linear. This is an area a lot of people, including my clients, get hung up on. They notice they are feeling better and better and then, wham, something happens and they feel as if they're back to square one. Rolfing clients I work with can experience being pain free for a few days, weeks, or months. Then they travel, get tired, are stressed, or must deal with something emotionally heavy, and suddenly, they're back in pain. Coaching clients I work with may gain confidence; they become bolder and clearer in their communication, and feel hot in their bodies. Then, someone says something harsh, or they see a triggering social media post, and suddenly, they want to hide under their covers and never speak up again.

I see this "wham" as a good thing. It is your body's way of letting you know the next shadow that is asking to be seen, that next layer that is ready to be uncovered and healed. It is your body letting you know that something is out of alignment. It would be overwhelming to feel all the hurt and pain and become aware of all your shadows at once. The layers of the onion peel away one at a time.

The growth process may have what feels like some ups and downs, but it is necessary. Instead of thinking we have fallen off the rails and are going backward, I think of them more as little divots, awareness signs to show us what we haven't fully been seeing.

The first coach I hired was a health coach, Rosie Bank, author of *Health Matters*. I remember making the investment to work with her for six months. It felt too expensive for me, but I knew I needed support around my body and eating. Looking back now, I realize how working with her was worth far more than what she charged.

On our calls together, I would always start sharing with some sort of judgment of how I had failed yet again that week, how I had overeaten this or that. Rosie had an acronym that doesn't roll off the tongue very well but one that I am quite fond of and continue to use personally and with my clients, MITRD: Moving in the Right Direction.

We don't tend to celebrate or acknowledge ourselves for the progress we have made, particularly our small steps in the right direction (toward the vision of what we desire and how we wish to feel). It is all too easy to keep trekking along, trying to be better.

Having witnesses in your celebrations magnifies them that much more. I am a huge fan of having a coach, therapist, mentor, or dear friend with whom you can share *all* of what you are going through. It can make all the difference to have someone who will hold your hand, see your blind spots, and support you in the next forward step of progress, someone who will celebrate along with you. Having a witness is huge! We all need to be seen in our pain as well as in our glory.

As I noted earlier, our minds are built to focus on what is not working. When we intentionally celebrate along the way, we can see the progress and forward steps we might have overlooked. Celebrating supports us in shifting our mind's pattern to see all that *is* working for us. It also helps us to feel lighter in the process toward what we desire in our lives and in our relationships.

When you are feeling emotional, frustrated, or even just comfortable, it is easy to not take the time to honor your progress. But by delighting in your forward steps, you can amplify them and support your momentum.

Start celebrating on the regular, my friend! I start each of my coaching client calls with celebrations. I also have them celebrate weekly, creating a feel-good ritual around it. I highly encourage you to start your own weekly celebrations and write them in your journal.

What are you celebrating this week? What shifts have you noticed internally? What old beliefs and stories have you released? How have you given extra love and attention to your body?

Anchor your celebration into your body. Feel the acknowledgment run through your energy field all the way into your skin and bones and the tissues in between.

It is *so* important to acknowledge your progress, to mark your achievements with joy!

Shadow Work

I've alluded to shadows a few times thus far in the book, but haven't explained what I fully mean, so let's go a bit deeper here. There are aspects of us that we accept and comfortably express. There are other aspects that we reject and suppress. We suppress certain parts of ourselves because at one time or another we received the message that they were not okay, that they were "bad," or that we weren't possibly good enough to claim them. These aspects are referred to as our "shadow" aspects. Carl Jung coined the term "the shadow self," which describes the unconscious parts of the personality that our conscious ego doesn't want to identify with.

The shadows are the parts of your personality you split off from. Your shadows are the parts of you you don't own. The problem is when you disown any part of you and push it away, it doesn't disappear; instead, it gets pushed into a dark corner of your unconscious world. They are always with you. When you feel triggered by another person and suddenly feel flooded with energy, that's a shadow. When you can allow in your shadows and integrate them, it will free up your life force.

We all have access to both ends of the spectrum of human emotion. We can be loving and fearful, aggressive and passive, defensive and open, and patient and impatient. We are all of them. We are independent and dependent. The full spectrum of the rainbow. We are all of the colors, the light and the dark. We are wise and stupid. We are open and closed off. Usually, the inner child chooses the colors, not our higher self. When you can integrate your shadows, it will give you access to so much more. So much more space. So much more choice.

We have what are called light shadows, those aspects that we tend to think of as "good," those aspects that are higher in vibration: love, openness, and patience. We also have what are called dark shadows. These are the aspects we typically think of as "bad" and are lower in vibration: aggression, defensiveness, and impatience.

If we don't acknowledge all aspects of ourselves, then those parts we have hidden away in dark corners will inevitably start clamoring for attention. The unconscious is constantly running through your system and your body. That is why we have spent so much time in this book working with limiting beliefs, those undesirable weeds in your garden, so that they no longer drive the show and you can release them.

You must be willing to look at that "sticky" place, that uncomfortable place, that place that feels icky. Going into the darkness, going into the ickiness is what will help you overcome the shadow. It will help you overcome the resistance. The moments when I used to feel the compulsion to overeat, as if something had taken over my body, there was a shadow I had suppressed that was really desiring to emerge.

Support

You are not meant to do this journey alone.

When our incredible mind overrides the show, sometimes asking for help can make us feel like we are weak. It takes courage to ask for help when you need it most. I see asking for help as a sign of strength.

We need to be able to feel the support of our own physical structure. We need to feel supported by those in our lives. We need hired support: bodyworkers, therapists, coaches, and delicious programs that help us grow. We need support we can rely on and surrender to. We need support to help hold us so we don't feel we have to do it all alone.

Have you experienced a difference with the support you feel in your body as you have moved through this book? In what areas of your life could you use more support?

Maybe you can relate to feeling you need to hide your thighs. Or perhaps distress around your body shows up differently. Maybe you have struggled with disordered eating, feeling too fat, feeling too thin. Whatever it is, if you find yourself apologizing for your body, if you feel insecure or ashamed in your body, please do the practices in this book and reach out to my team or someone you know for support. As a woman, your power and your confidence reside in your body. Beginning to learn to connect to the vast wisdom your body offers you is not only the fast track to success, it also leads to long-term results and fulfillment. Your story, your pattern, does not have to continue. You can feel amazing in your body!

PRACTICE

Bringing It all Together

With this activity, we are uniting all the practices you have done so far in the book.

To start, find your How to Sit with Natural Alignment posture. See how soft your body can be here when your bones are aligned. Bring your breath into your belly and lower back. Start to shift your attention into the lower half of your body.

Come to the center point of your pelvis. Breathe here for a few long moments, gifting yourself the feeling of being grounded and calm. Come up into your heart and let it soften, allowing it to surrender into the structural and energetic support of your pelvis. Feel the front and back of your heart space. See if you can bring to unison your heart and womb, breathing in and out together in each space.

Now anchor into your vertical core, the center point of your head, heart, and womb space. Luxuriate here for a while. Connecting with this energetic vertical space will naturally help your physical posture improve and be more upright.

Next, feel that core as the inner filament of a light bulb, which has turned on because you are aware of it. Let that light expand at least an arm's length all around you. That is your energy field, your energetic presence. Feel the malleable edge of your field. Keep circulating your energy back and through you. When it hits the border of your field, it gets to bounce back to and through you. It is all for you.

From this space, repeat any affirmations you have been working with. Feel the containment. Feel the spaciousness. Feel the yumminess.

CHAPTER 12

My Body, the Gift

When I think about my body now, a smile comes to my face. I feel a delightful jolt of energy surge up through my spine. My body is now my home. It is my sanctuary. It is my greatest teacher and my most loyal friend.

One of the most important keys in my journey toward continuously loving and accepting my body is slowing down. Decelerating the train of resistant, negative thought, and relaxing back and in instead of popping up and out and being driven by habituation. From that slowing down, space is created to process and experience my emotions, to be with me, my desires and needs.

Through my own journey, I found the sweetness of life. It fascinates me that I can have a day of feeling lumpy and too big and then, two days later, feel incredible in my body. What has happened? My body has not changed size or appearance; instead, my mental and emotional state has changed. That is what has me feeling so good.

And you? As you continue beyond the pages of this book, how will you continue to make the changes that'll have you feeling fantastic?

Here it is, short and sweet:

First, notice and then question a thought or judgment. When limiting beliefs come in, question them. Is it true you are too big, weak, not enough, fake, flawed, too much, or not worthy? Then ask more deeply, can you absolutely know that what you're thinking is true? Who would you be without that thought? Question the truth and validity of *all* limiting beliefs. Start to invite in these questions when negative thoughts show up.

Remember the garden of your subconscious mind? Remember to weed it of thoughts that trick you into thinking you are less than.

Who you are at your core is an incredible being. You are perfect. You came into this life to do great things, not to feel stuck in the constraints of your mind. Use your limiting beliefs for your benefit. Learn from them. Gain insight. Discover where their roots came from so you can heal. Don't give up or give in to them.

Next, show up fully. This does not mean you need to show up as your best or ideal self. It means allowing in the full spectrum of your humanity. Instead of resisting when you are feeling tired, sad, lonely, or frustrated and trying to suppress it, showing up fully means accepting and allowing in what is present.

Showing up fully requires that we feel fully. Sometimes, clients of mine worry about fully feeling what is present internally. They worry they might get stuck in story or numbed with insecurities. It can feel easier to bypass into positivity and put on a fake front versus committing to feel *all* of your feelings.

My clients fear that feeling fully is going to affect their work, so they need to compartmentalize. However, the truth is, the more we continue to build a foundational anchor inside our bodies, specifically by continually inhabiting our womb space, the more we will have the capacity to be with what we are feeling (the pain, agitation, anger, sadness) while still being fully present with work, loved ones, and life. Your compartmentalizing is not serving anyone. You can feel deep levels of frustration or grief while still feeling gratitude and appreciation for what you have, for being here in this lifetime, and for being exactly where you are.

Maybe you need to lead a group or give a presentation and you're not feeling great. First, let that be okay. Allowing yourself to feel upset doesn't mean you're going to share your dirty laundry with everyone or that you are going to bomb the presentation. Instead, you are inviting in your full presence, not rejecting parts of you, which in turn will enable you to be more magnetic and feel more confident.

Showing up fully by allowing yourself to feel fully allows and invites in your humanness. When you do this, you offer a gift to those around you as you are giving permission to others to be themselves more fully as they are in this moment.

And then there's manifesting. Often, when it comes to setting goals and making things happen, the emphasis is on what you want externally. To access that external desire, you are likely to focus on mentally pepping yourself up into a positive space. There is talk of "overcoming your mind" and to only think positively.

Though these concepts are important, when you leave your body out of the equation, your vision takes *much* longer to come to fruition.

Look directly at the places where your mind and body are out of alignment and lack integrity. This, my friends, will take you directly into your pain, directly into the uncomfortable shadow places you tend to avoid. But you must feel that and move through it to experience your fullest vision of the desires that await on the other side. The nervous system is the brain of the body and weaves through us in a beautiful way. When you embody your vision, when you can feel it through every cell while simultaneously having your thoughts align around it, that is where your true manifesting power is.

Embodiment practices like the ones in this book are *key.* Coming home to your body is what is going to allow you to feel safe while you are experiencing the discomfort of going into the unknown. Anytime you anchor into your womb space, you are retraining your nervous system that you are safe. A gentle exhale through your mouth with your breath caressing your lips as it leaves your mouth, lets your nervous system know you are safe. It is okay to relax. It is okay to settle as you actively bring up pain or discomfort that lurks in the hidden grooves of your fascia.

Get more comfortable in the uncertainty. If you can listen to the call of your heart and body and say to life, "I'm going to trust that all will work out," then magic happens. Softening happens, through your physical tissue as well as in your mental and emotional sphere.

The Journey Continues

This journey toward loving your body is not a journey that is necessarily ever "done." There are layers, chapters, and sections to the evolving story. We live in a culture that is fixated on external validation. When we ease up and loosen the reins of control and stop trying to prove ourselves to others, we put ourselves back in the saddle. Suddenly, more energy is freed up to put toward what you really care about and what fulfills you: relationships, family, service, community, the environment, your mission.

You may be thinking, "Yeah, but my life won't really change that much if I begin to accept and love my body a little more." Maybe you are feeling overwhelmed and exhausted from previous efforts. Think instead of a ripple effect. One small, seemingly insignificant droplet of water as it lands upon a large pond. The ripples it creates grow in size as they spread, touching an incredible amount of space on their way to the edges where the water meets the land. Your ripple, your impact, reaches farther than you may ever know.

Then, when you come into relationship, you are connected to yourself and anchored into your truth. This is what deepens connection and grows stronger, more fulfilling relationships.

So, why does it matter to me that you feel a flicker of change in the way you relate to you body? Connection and love for one's body naturally leads to more understanding, compassion, and inclusiveness. It brings us together instead of dividing us further apart. Loving and connecting with your body creates internal space, which allows us to hear opposing viewpoints and beliefs. Loving our bodies enables us to not get stuck in rigidity and narrow thinking. It gives us a chance to have discussion, connection, and unification.

May this book act as one significant ripple in perpetuating the chain of healing around female bodies and body image.

The journey toward loving your body ever more deeply continues.

PRACTICE

Make It Your Own

Now you get to do what feels good to you. You get to take what felt most enjoyable for you from the practices and make it your own. My invitation with this practice is to bring your power, your ownership, and your leadership back to yourself and into your own body. Your body is your greatest guide. This is an opportunity with the tools you have learned thus far, to see what kind of practice your body would like to do.

A bit of guidance so you don't feel completely lost. On your own (or through listening to the online guided meditation for Chapter Seven), run through your powerful centers: womb space, heart space, and energy field. Being aware of your expansive containment, do your *abhyanga* (self-massage). It is such a gift to give yourself this. Go slowly.

As you massage yourself, say your affirmations feeling their juicy vibrations. Spend longer on the areas of your body you have historically hated. Notice if you feel different in relationship to these areas of your body than when you first began this book and journey. As you massage these parts of yourself, are you able to experience pleasure here? Feel your own internal energetic space as you do so.

At the end of this, take your sweet, precious time and sit for at least five minutes in silence, rooted in your womb space and expanded out through your energy field. The above order is simply a suggestion. You get to decide what order you do the practices in; you get to choose what practices you choose to do. You get to add in other practices that support you in coming back into your body and into yourself.

This is you reclaiming your body. This is you giving your love and power back to yourself.

ABOUT THE AUTHOR

Emily Wishall

Emily Wishall knows what it is like to feel insecure, ashamed, tired, and constricted in her body. Through her own journey of transformation, she has been able to better understand and help her clients overcome their own limitations and has been passionate about supporting women on the path to loving their bodies. An Embodiment Coach, Certified Rolfer, Art of Feminine Presence Teacher, and Certified Animal Flow Instructor, Emily graduated from the University of Kansas with a Bachelor's Degree in Exercise Science.

Through her signature coaching process, Emily helps her clients to release shame and the old postural and mental patterns keeping them stuck, small, and limited, guiding her clients to feel more confident, energized, and at home in their bodies.

In developing her unique approach to body love, Emily has received training in specialized topics ranging from craniosacral work, the neuroscience behind chronic pain, functional methods from an osteopathic perspective, a year-long Feminine Leadership Mastery Program, and Active Fascial Unwinding.

Emily lives in Boulder, Colorado. In her free time, she likes to be in nature, whether hiking on the trails or camping, leisure trail running, skiing, or reading a book in the sun. She spends most of her time with her sweet dog, Tula Rose, and her family who live nearby (she is the youngest of seven and currently has ten nieces and nephews).

To learn more about Emily and her work, you can visit her website at www.WishallWellness.com.

Acknowledgments

I have so many people to thank it is hard to know where to start, so I guess I'll start with my main bud, Tula Rose, my sweet pup who cuddled with me as I wrote every single page of this book.

A special deep bow of gratitude to my amazing editor Gabrielle Idlet. She was the first to read my manuscript, the version that I referred to as ". . . a very, very rough, rough first draft that was shit." Thank you, Gabi, for getting my work, for seeing the value even when I couldn't.

Thank you to my book designer, Melinda Martin, for her beautiful cover design and for seeing my vision for this book so clearly.

Thank you to all my dear clients, with your continued questions, genuine excitement, and encouragement about this book.

Thank you, Rachael Jayne Groover, for creating the Art of Feminine Presence work. For holding me in the year-long container of your Feminine Leadership Mastery Program. You saw in me what I knew to be true but couldn't yet access.

Dawn Todd, thank you for your belief in me since early on in my Rolfing practice. You always knew I would do more, and your belief and clarity in me has meant more than you can know. Thank you for continuing to be my coach.

Thank you to so many of my sweet, supportive friends: Erica Sigel, Anne Chernick, and Sara Jess to name a few. My dear, loving, constant family, thank you for always being there for me, for always showing up, for always loving me.

To my sensual dance teachers, Ali, Jen, and Liz, who see me move through all of it and grace me with your wondrous reflections and insight.

I have such a long list of gratitude to express to my healers, coaches, and teachers over the years. The people who held support for me, where I got to be messy, where I got to be held, and for you to consistently reflect my Truth: Rosie Bank, Tawney Avonne, Macy Matarazzo, Kari Mitchell, Jeff Howard, Lily Calfee, and Anne Kirvan to name a few.

And to the people along my journey thus far, the ones I've met in weekend-long trainings and workshops, reflecting back to me my power, my future, my potential when I could not see it nor feel it. When I felt flat and unworthy, you saw Me. I can't begin to thank you enough or express the warmth in my heart I feel for you for this.

Thank You

May you experience reverence and love for this beautiful body of yours, dear reader.

As I feel my wish for you, I feel my heart and my womb light up. I am hopeful and excited about the potential you contain, what is possible for you and your life, when you begin the journey of learning to love your body.

My wish is that you feel confident and happy in your body, so you can relax and enjoy just being you. May you do the things you most desire to do in this life. May you experience more allowance, more permission, more grace.

May you develop a genuine love for the simple contact of touching your own skin. It can be electrifying. This is where the juice of life is.

Remember, support is here for you. If you haven't already, download the free guided practice that goes along with Chapter Seven. Continue to utilize it. Go to www.wishallwellness.com/radical-embodiment-free and enter your email and the free practice will be delivered to your inbox. You can also learn more about my community and how you can receive support to hold you on the days those limiting beliefs try to suck you down with their powerful roots. Be aware that the more consistent you are with the practices, the more you will be able to sense and feel and start a ripple effect of positive change.

I'd love to hear from you. Your reviews on Amazon will help others find this work, so if you are inspired, thank you for leaving a review. Reach out to learn more about my private coaching and community and how you can receive the support you need by going to www.wishallwellness.com.

Made in USA - Kendallville, IN
46149_9781951692186
07.15.2022 1342